AMERICAN GOTHIC

W. W. NORTON & COMPANY

NEW YORK ★ LONDON

★

A Life of
America's Most
Famous Painting

AMERICAN
GOTHIC

STEVEN BIEL

Copyright © 2005 by Steven Biel

For information about permission to reproduce selections
from this book, write to Permissions, W. W. Norton &
Company, Inc., 500 Fifth Avenue, New York, NY 10110

Manufacturing by Courier Westford
Book design by Judith Stagnitto Abbate
Production manager: Anna Oler

Library of Congress Cataloging-in-Publication Data
Biel, Steven, 1960–
American Gothic: a life of America's most famous
painting / Steven Biel.—1st ed.
p. cm.
Includes bibliographical references and index.
ISBN 0-393-05912-X (hardcover)
1. Wood, Grant, 1891–1942. American Gothic. 2. Wood,
Grant, 1891–1942—Public opinion. 3. National charac-
teristics, American, in art. I. Title.
ND237.W795A66 2005
759.13—dc22   2005004726

W. W. Norton & Company, Inc.
500 Fifth Avenue, New York, N.Y. 10110
www.wwnorton.com

W. W. Norton & Company Ltd.
Castle House, 75/76 Wells Street, London W1T 3QT

1 2 3 4 5 6 7 8 9 0

To Olivia, Jacob, and Jean,
and to my colleagues and students
in History and Literature

★

CONTENTS

ACKNOWLEDGMENTS

This book took longer to write than it could have. I thankfully blame my family and my job.

We live in a Victorian Gothic house, but I've resisted the urge to pose Jake and Olivia in front of it and use the picture as an illustration. It's only fair, Jake, that Olivia gets listed first in the dedication. She wasn't here yet for *Down with the Old Canoe*, and you still have two dedications to her one. Olivia, I'm not going to exclude Jake to even things up. Mom has three, so if you're going to complain, take it up with her.

History and Literature has been described as the "happy valley" of Harvard, and it has been for me. I work with inspiring teachers, scholars, students, and administrators. I'm grateful to all of them. It's been a particular honor to work closely with Marcia Dambry, Cynthia Martin, Chris Churchill, Claire Sammon, Patricia Lynch, John O'Keefe, Shirley Thompson, Stephen Kargère, Tim McCarthy, Charitini Douvaldzi, Laura Johnson, Andy Romig, Billy Weitzel, Jeanne Follansbee Quinn, Karen Flood, Dan Donoghue, Stephen Greenblatt, and Homi Bhabha.

Ruth Feldstein, Jona Hansen, Jane Kamensky, Stephen Mihm, Mark Peterson, Jeanne Follansbee Quinn, John Stauffer, John Thomas, Michael Willrich, and the members of the graduate American history seminar at Brown in the fall of 2003 read drafts and gave me great suggestions. A captive audience of History and Literature sophomores listened to me talk about *American Gothic* and shared their sharp insights. A noncaptive audience at a Harvard Humanities Center colloquium did the same.

Lots of friends and colleagues passed along *American Gothic* parodies and collectors' items, from "Alf" comics to a flip-book that morphs *American Gothic* into Munch's *The Scream*. (It's called *Gothic Scream*, and VAGA, the Visual Artists and Galleries Association, hasn't been able to track down the perpetrators.) If I listed names, I'd be certain to leave out someone. I hope that a general thank you is OK.

Alfred Gescheidt talked with me about his marvelous parodies. Len Glasser and Vincent Cafarelli talked with me about their hilarious Country Corn Flakes commercial, and Amid Amidi sent me a copy of it. Bruce Thiher talked with me about the famous house he lived in. Robert Panzer talked with me about protecting the rights of Nan Wood Graham's estate. Sean Ploen and Inna Fayenson talked with me about copyright law.

Sarah Potvin found me H. L. Mencken's letter to Grant Wood. They were all very generous. So were the curators and archivists who helped me with my research: Denise Mahoney, Daniel Schulman, Courtney Graham Donnell, and Bart Ryckbosch at the Art Institute of Chicago; Christopher Whittington and Teri Coate-Saal at the Cedar Rapids Museum of Art; Michelle Robinson at the Davenport (now Figge) Museum of Art; Amy Cary and Kathryn Hodson in Special Collections at the University of Iowa Library; and the staffs of the Smithsonian's Archives of American Art and the Beinecke Library at Yale. Elizabeth Pierson's careful copyediting saved me from some embarrassing mistakes. Alessandra Bastagli and Vanessa Levine-Smith skillfully helped guide the manuscript to publication.

Michele Rubin is an extraordinary agent. Alane Salierno Mason is a brilliant editor. I'm glad that I got to work with both of them again.

AMERICAN
GOTHIC

THE "ORIGINAL"

I t didn't occur to me at first to look at the house from anywhere but straight on. I glimpsed it as soon as it came into view as I drove out Route 16 (the "American Gothic Parkway") from the center of Eldon, Iowa, curved along Railroad, Willie, and Finney Streets, and turned left on American Gothic Street. But I didn't look at it until I got out of my car after observing the arrow for "American Gothic House Parking." Following these directions put me directly in front of the house, where any tourists who find themselves in Eldon would expect to end up. (I happened to be there alone that day.) Even without the directions, the image instructs us

The American Gothic House, Eldon, Iowa, from the usual angle. [Steven Biel]

how to position ourselves before the "original." We've seen it so many times that we know where to stand. "American Gothic House," reads the sign next to the parking lot. "Built in 1881–82":

> You are standing in front of the "American Gothic" house that Grant Wood used as the backdrop for his world-famous portrait of the stern figures. Thousands of parodies of the painting have been created over the past half century. Now it's your turn to pose for your own photograph! The building has always been a private residence except when it was briefly used as a candy and novelty store. Downstairs there are three rooms and a bathroom, upstairs there are two bedrooms each with its own gothic window. In recent

years the house has undergone extensive preservation
to maintain it as it appears in Wood's 1930 painting.
The house's historic value is its exterior appearance—
the way Wood saw it when sketching the background
for his famous "American Gothic." The interior is too
small and fragile for public tours. The house is
leased to a private resident caretaker. The American
Gothic House was placed on the National Register of
Historic Places in 1974. Carl E. Smith donated the
house to the State of Iowa as a historic site in 1991.
The State Historical Society of Iowa owns and manages the site. An education center is being planned
for the site.

A different perspective, from the corner of American Gothic and Burton Streets.
[Steven Biel]

"The way Wood saw it." The sign suggests that we can't see it otherwise—and probably wouldn't want to anyway.

Perversely, then, I walk to the corner of American Gothic and Burton Streets, to look at it from the right. I eagerly head up Burton, propelled by the realization that *there is a backside to the house*. I take photographs from behind, standing on the mowed and browning lawn. In the middle ground, a clothesline is strung across two crucifixes that point upward toward the second, rear gothic window—the one that doesn't appear in the painting. There is a screened porch, patio furniture, a compressor for the central air. I have defied the sign and entered into three dimensions.

Grant Wood saw the house in August 1930 on a car ride with John Sharp, an eighteen-year-old Eldon native and aspiring painter. Wood came to Eldon because of an experiment in artistic outreach. That summer, Edward Rowan, the young director of the Little Gallery in Cedar Rapids, decided to extend his efforts at promoting community fine arts to a smaller town by renting a five-room house on West Elm Street for exhibitions and art classes. "Mr. Rowan," reported the *Ottumwa Courier*, "announces that the extension work is done to show that the small midwestern community, entirely isolated from certain contacts, will yet respond most heartily to them when the opportunity for appreciation of the fine arts is given." Like Cedar Rapids, where Rowan arrived in 1928 from graduate school at Harvard's Fogg Museum with a grant from the Carnegie Foundation and the sponsorship of the American Federation of Arts, Eldon responded to the experiment in the booster spirit. The *Eldon Forum* called the exhibitions, some by outsiders and others by local artists, "an unusual treat," and Rowan related that the gallery had attracted more than a thousand visitors from twenty-two Iowa communities, many of them from Eldon itself or the neighboring town of Ottumwa, despite the hundred-degree temperatures of an August heat wave in Iowa. "One old woman," Rowan exulted to a Cedar Rapids friend, "is getting more kick out of the gallery than she has had in the last forty-five years."[1]

The Eldon experiment was especially good for Sharp and Wood. A wealthy Ottumwa native, now a New Yorker, heard about Sharp's exhibition from friends and sponsored his study at New York's Art Students' League. (" 'Johnny Sharp could always draw pretty good,' they say at Eldon now, for Johnny is making a name for himself in New York art circles," the *Des Moines Register* heralded the following winter.) Wood made a painting of the "unprepossessing" house that served as the Eldon gallery, but when Rowan showed it at a convention of art patrons "no one apparently saw anything in it, since Mr. Wood had not yet established his national reputation." Rowan didn't have to wait long to boast about the Eldon experiment's role in Wood's second painting of an Eldon house. "It is noteworthy to recall that the particular house which prompted Mr. Wood to create his 'American Gothic' was discovered by him on a visit to our Eldon experiment," Rowan told the American Federation of Arts convention in Brooklyn in May 1931. Parenthetically, "in fairness," he added "that the idea had been revolving in the artist's mind for several years—but needed the particular impetus which he found in Eldon."[2]

"Stop!" Wood's sister Nan imagined him exclaiming from the passenger's seat to Sharp behind the wheel. "There's a house I want to use." He was fascinated by the Carpenter, or Steamboat, Gothic style of midwestern houses such as this: perhaps, as the art historian and Wood biographer Wanda Corn has written, "because of its compactness and its emphatic design—particularly the verticals in the board-and-batten construction and the Gothic window, prominently placed in the gable"; perhaps, as the *Cedar Rapids Gazette* and Wood's first biographer speculated, because of the "unstructural absurdity," "the false taste, the borrowed pretentiousness" of "a style originally copied from stone Gothic churches in Europe" and applied "to flimsy frame houses in America."[3]

He painted the Eldon house in its front yard, in oil on paperboard he had brought along for the trip. In the sketch, weeds and a young tree occupy the foreground. Scratches in the paint give the impression that the tree is blowing in a breeze. A short ladder is propped against one of the porch posts. The sun glints off the lower right pane of the gothic window. Tall trees overhang the house on both sides. Here already was the direction from which we will inevitably (or almost inevitably) view the house. Here too was the narrowing of the gable and the elongation of the window that Wood carried over into the final painting and that made the lanky house more real than the relatively chubby model.[4]

The foreground quickly changed. In a pencil sketch that he did on the unmarked side of a white envelope at the breakfast table back home in Cedar Rapids, Wood replaced the weeds and the tree with rough though quite recognizable versions of the female and male figures we know so well, tall and

Back from Eldon in Cedar Rapids, Wood did a pencil drawing with the figures in place and the title "American Gothic." The man was holding a rake instead of a pitchfork. [© Estate of Grant Wood/Licensed by VAGA, New York, NY]

thin like the stretched gable and window, she with a white collar and brooch, he collarless with overalls and a black coat and holding a long tool, at this point a rake. Wood called the sketch "American Gothic."

Just as we know how to pose for our parodies, Wood could

base his picture on an older set of visual clichés. In the late nineteenth century, pioneers posed solemnly in front of their sod houses or dugouts, later their frame houses, often with their most important possessions, for portrait photographers who made an uncertain living on the homesteading frontier. One of Solomon D. Butcher's photographs of Nebraska—it's unlikely that Wood actually saw it—intriguingly features a homesteader named John Curry, standing rigidly with his wife in front of their sod house, grasping an upward-pointing pitchfork in his hand. (The Nebraska State Historical Society notes that this 1886 photograph is now sometimes referred to, anachronistically, as "Nebraska Gothic.") In other Butcher portraits, the farmer holds a scythe or a saw, harking back,

Solomon D. Butcher's "Nebraska Gothic," the John Curry sod house near West Union, Nebraska. [Nebraska State Historical Society Photograph Collections]

Wanda Corn explains, to "an even older painting convention" in which men and women "held objects appropriate to their status and occupation." Such formal poses were customary at a time before snapshots, when standing or sitting for the photographer, even an itinerant frontier photographer, was a special and serious occasion. The sternness of the homesteaders' pose, like the "permanence" of the photograph itself, served as a poignant counterstatement to the precariousness of their existence. In *American Gothic*'s play on these photographs, forty or fifty years later, this pioneer severity would take on different connotations.[5]

Wood told Nan and his mother, with whom he lived in a converted carriage house at 5 Turner Alley, behind his friend David Turner's new mortuary, that he knew a woman and a man "who would just be perfect" to pose as the pair. "I think Dr. McKeeby (the family dentist) would be an ideal model for the man," Nan remembered him saying. "He has a long narrow face. I have in mind a model for the woman, but I'm afraid she would be mad if I asked her to pose. Women want to look pretty, but I don't like to paint pretty women." Nan asked, "What's the matter with me?" Then, according to her 1944 remembrance, "Grant studied my face for a moment then exclaimed, 'Why yes. Of course, you'll do. You're sure you won't mind? Your face is too round, but I can stretch it out long.'" (In Nan's posthumously published biography of her brother, she recalled his words as less delicate: "Your face is too fat, but I can slim it down.") Byron McKeeby evidently required more convincing. Wood explained that "he wanted a face showing integrity from a man with a sense of humor"—a man "who would not rebel at the distortion that might be necessary to carry out his theme." Assured by his patient that "the painting was in no manner intended to be a portrait," the dentist consented.[6]

Nan posed at home at 5 Turner Alley. McKeeby posed at his dental office. He and Nan did not pose together. "Grant assured us both," said Nan,

> that when he finished the painting, no one would ever recognize us. He told me to slick down my hair and part it in the middle and asked me to make an apron trimmed with rickrack, a trim that was out of style and unavailable in the stores. I ripped some off Mother's old dresses, and after the painting made its debut, rickrack made a comeback. Grant was responsible for a rickrack revival.

The cameo was also Mother's.[7]

Wood painted *American Gothic* in three months. He started with a thirty- by twenty-five-inch piece of relatively cheap beaver board, made from compressed wood pulp and used in construction for walls and partitions. He applied a white foundation, now yellowed where it wasn't covered with other paint (especially in the boards of the house), and drew an outline of the picture in black. Then he filled it in, laying thicker textures on the house and overalls, lighter textures in more delicate strokes on the faces. Photomacrographs reveal a finger print just below the left lens (our right) of the man's glasses. The strokes also thicken on the left shoulder of his black suit coat, and Wood curled the left lapel with some gray shading. White touches on the browns of the man's collar button made the gold gleam. Dark brown strokes and scratches created his wattle and the contours of his face. On the dark brown of the woman's apron, art historians James S. Horns and Helen Mar Parkin explain, Wood layered light brown around the white dots and circles of the print pattern. In a few spots (the man's eyebrow, for example, "where a black brush stroke of paint has broken into small dots"), Wood had trouble with his careful layering. He painted over a chimney on the house's left addition that had survived from his first sketch, changed the second gothic window that he'd added in the envelope sketch back to a door on the addition, introduced details such as potted plants on the porch, a rolled-up blind above the door, the edge of a red barn on the right, and in the background under the sky the puffy, rounded, highly stylized trees that would reappear in many of his subsequent paintings.[8]

He also turned the rake into a three-pronged pitchfork that doubled the design of the wrinkles in the man's overalls and mirrored the gothic window in the gable. The pitchfork glistened silver with white highlights on grays and blacks, capturing the sunshine that angled down at forty-five degrees and cast a shadow under the gable and on the porch's clapboards. Dashes of light blue, white, and black produced the pitchfork pattern on the overalls. Later, in response to complaints that "he didn't know anything about pitchforks, since all of 'em have 4 prongs"—and to conjectures "that the prongs had deep religious or phallic significance"—he said that the pitchfork he painted really did have three prongs. I heard a docent at the Art Institute of Chicago try to clear up the controversy by explaining that it's a hay fork, not a pitchfork. The Scotts Company's gardenadvice.com confirms that three-tined forks are usually used for working with hay.[9]

Wood signed and dated the painting in light blue on the black and dark blue below the waist of the overalls:

GRANT

WOOD

1930

Even before he started painting *American Gothic*, he planned to enter it in the Art Institute of Chicago's Forty-Third Annual Exhibition of American Paintings and Sculpture. At the exhibition's opening reception on October 30, 1930, the *Chicago Post* reported, "society leaders, wealthy art patrons and plain bohemian art fans swarmed in a vast throng" to hear the winners announced. *American Gothic* won the Norman Wait Harris Bronze Medal and $300 (about $3,200 today). The silver medal and $500 were awarded to Guy Pène du Bois for *Valley of the Chevreuse*. Louis Ritman received the gold medal and $1,500 for *Jullien*. The museum's Friends of American Art then bought Wood's painting for $300, and it became part of the permanent collection.

Years later a former trustee of the Art Institute claimed that he had intervened with the chairman of the exhibition's jury, which had initially rejected *American Gothic*. As a member of the committee that oversaw the prizes, he felt it his duty to look at all the paintings the jury had seen. He quickly went over the rejected canvases and, "thinking that the jury had inadvertently overlooked it," came back to the chairman carrying *American Gothic*. "I see you brought in that comic valentine," the chairman said. A "little indignant," the trustee told the jury how much he liked the painting and urged them to give it a prize. Then he bought the painting and convinced his friend, the president of the Friends of American Art, to pay him back for it and accept it for the museum. He didn't reveal any of this—not wanting to hurt the jury chairman's feelings or reputation or to cast doubt on his judgment—until he intervened again on the painting's behalf, this time in the 1950s to prevent the loan of *American Gothic* for an exhibition in the Soviet Union, where it would, he feared, "be exposed to bad handling and the radical changes in temperature." Only then did he confess his "sentimental interest" in the painting as "its first owner (for a few hours)."[10]

An image familiar to almost everyone might have been seen by almost nobody. A painting that became a national icon nearly got sent back, barely noticed, to Iowa.

Pose for your own photograph," the sign reads. We need no further instructions. We know exactly how to position ourselves, how to compose our faces and bodies, what to pretend to hold in our hand. Unfortunately, I am alone and, respectful of the sign's admonition that there are no public tours and that it is occupied by a *private* resident caretaker, I have nobody to pose with or to take my picture. Some people in Eldon are aware of this problem. "That house is one of our best attractions," said Iowa state senator Donald E. Gettings. "The big problem is that a lot of people just can't find it."

Unlike the Iowa tourism prophet in the 1989 movie *Field of Dreams* ("If you build it, they will come"), Gettings knew that word of mouth has its limits as a marketing tool: "We need to get some billboards up, some brochures and bus tours rolling in—we'll be right up there with Mt. Rushmore as a tourist draw." A professional photographer, skillfully arranging the tourists with pitchforks, could capture and sell *American Gothic* memories.[11]

But the boosters had other problems besides showing visitors how to get there. The house's owner, Carl Smith of Cleveland, Ohio, wasn't willing to sell, even though in 1986 the Iowa legislature had agreed with Gettings to use lottery money to buy it for the state. Smith's concern was that his tenants, Kelly and Kelly Haynes and their children, Michelle and Amy, wouldn't have anywhere else to live. They couldn't even afford the fifty dollars rent he charged them, Smith said. "Their parents pay that." In February 1986, the *San Francisco Examiner* posed Mr. Haynes, a "laconic 26-year-old weed cutter," with one of his daughters in front of the house to dramatize the first in a series of articles about America's farm crisis. "The American Gothic is unemployed," the article intoned. "He no longer has the pitchfork but as he stands in front of Grant Wood's celebrated farm home here, he remains a metaphor for a way of life." A year and a half later, *People* magazine posed the entire Haynes family in front of the house and quoted an "agitated Mrs. Haynes" pleading: "The state better be prepared to find us another place to live. They just better. They can't just throw us out." The idea of helping "generate income in the depressed farm area" by boosting tourism ran into the problem of displacing tenants who didn't have the income to relocate.[12]

Before Carl Smith's parents, Seldon and Myra, bought the house at a "distress sale" in 1942, it had belonged to the Howards and before that to the Joneses, who owned it when

*The Haynes family in front of their rental house in
1987. [Taro Yamasaki]*

Wood saw it in 1930. (Vernon "Whitey" Jones, the grandson of
these Joneses and owner of the Jones Cafe and Rocket Room
in Eldon, was skeptical about the 1980s' boosterism. "We
could handle a million people here," he said, "if you give us a
million years.") Seldon and Myra rented the house to Seldon's
brother P. W., who had been living in Ottumwa and "had an
alcohol problem," according to Carl Smith's sister. P. W. lived

there from 1942 until his death in 1954, and his widow stayed on until she died in 1965. The house was unoccupied from then until Carl Smith inherited it in 1971. Starting in 1945, there was a series of unsuccessful efforts, sometimes including Nan, to turn the house into a museum or otherwise preserve it. By the time Carol and Bill Wilkinson moved in in 1977 ("with their dog Wimpy, who loved posing for pictures on the porch or looking out the windows"), the house was in bad shape. Somebody had fired a bullet into a bedroom wall. "The grass grew up high during the summer," a visitor to the then-vacant house observed in the early 1970s;

> a woodpecker has pecked a hole in one of the porch columns, and vandals have broken out some of the windows now replaced with tin. Black roll roofing has been used to cover the curling shake shingles, and weather has turned the white paint a dull gray. Inside, the plaster has crumbled; pieces of faded wallpaper have cracked and fallen off.[13]

The State Historical Society was reluctant to assume title when in 1991 Carl Smith decided, at the urging of Wood's former secretary and his few surviving students, to donate the house in honor of the centennial of Wood's birth instead of waiting until Smith died. ("[T]his would be more fun," he explained at the ceremony celebrating the donation.) By then, the Hayneses had left for greener pastures, but the house was "on the verge of collapse," recalls Bruce Thiher, until recently Eldon's postmaster and the house's resident caretaker. John Fitzpatrick, the arts coordinator for the Cedar Rapids schools and a Wood devotee, had to "grease the wheels" by making a personal appeal to Iowa governor Terry Branstad. Eldonians then had to fight off an attempt to move the house to Living History Farms just outside Des Moines. In 1992, the house was lifted and stabilized, a basement dug, new utilities installed, fresh paint applied. The legislature approved $150,000 for the education center that the sign mentions, but Eldonians worried about who would pay to operate and maintain it. They voted the pro-education center mayor and town council out of office in 1999. In 2004, the state again came up with $150,000 from casino revenues, but the town has to raise matching funds—an unlikely prospect given the area's ongoing economic and population decline.[14]

The carriage house behind the Turner Mortuary where Wood painted *American Gothic* has fared better. The funeral home's current owners donated the 5 Turner Alley building to the Cedar Rapids Museum of Art in 2003, and the museum raised funds to restore the upstairs studio and create a first-floor visitors center.[15]

The boosters defeated, tourism in Eldon remains very modest. It might have received a spur from the arrival of Roseanne and Tom Arnold, who bought an 850-acre cornfield nearby in 1991 and planned to build a 26,000-square-foot mansion that *People*, posing the celebrity couple à la *American Gothic*, of course, called "an Iowa Xanadoozy." "It has Victorian turrets, but with a farmhouse feel in how the rooms go together, and Gothic-like winding staircases and dark wood," said Roseanne. "It's awesome." But this gothic house was never built. Roseanne and Tom split up, the cornfield was leased to a farmer, the "loose meat" restaurant they had planned for Eldon never opened, and the local community college took over the property. Courtney Graham, who toured the

Roseanne and Tom Arnold at the site of their planned mansion near Eldon.
[Photo by Bob Modersohn. Copyright 1991, The Des Moines Register and
Tribune Company. Reprinted with permission.]

area in 1996 and published her journal on the Internet, visited
the Arnolds' cornfield and the American Gothic House, which
underwhelmed her. "It was just a little white house that someone lives in," she wrote, "hidden behind a city maintenance
building. You'd think it would be in a fancier area or be a big
tourist attraction."[16]

I have to agree, having visited Eldon twice, that it is "just a little white house"—"a pretty ordinary house for that part of the country," as Courtney Donnell of the Art Institute of Chicago points out, with the same vertical clapboards and battening as the Herbert Hoover birthplace in West Branch, which is much closer to Cedar Rapids and Iowa City and which Wood painted a year after *American Gothic*. Then again, with the right kind of publicity, the ordinary can sometimes be transformed into the "big tourist attraction" that Courtney Graham expected. In Don DeLillo's novel *White Noise*, two characters follow the signs to "THE MOST PHOTOGRAPHED BARN IN AMERICA." "We walked along a cowpath to the slightly elevated spot set aside for viewing and photographing. All the people had cameras; some had tripods, telephoto lenses, filter kits. A man in a booth sold postcards and slides—pictures of the barn taken from the elevated spot." Amid several long silences, one character remarks:

> No one sees the barn. . . . Once you've seen the signs about the barn, it becomes impossible to see the barn. . . . We see only what the others see. The thousands who were here in the past, those who will come in the future. We've agreed to be part of a collective perception. This literally colors our vision. A religious experience in a way, like all tourism.

Probably by now there have been thousands of tourists at the American Gothic House, though Thiher concedes that the only people who have found it so far are the ones, like me, "who already have an interest." We are similarly absorbed into a collective perception. We know the right spot for photographs. "We can't get outside the aura," as DeLillo's delighted tourist observes.[17] Maybe there was something to Donald Gettings's vision of billboards, brochures, and bus tours; maybe with the full force of marketing it wouldn't be a pretty ordinary house; maybe this house that we've seen so often even if we haven't been there could also have become the most photographed.

Grant Wood arrived at the Eldon house and *American Gothic* via the archetypal modern pilgrimage from farm to metropolis, except that in his case the journey brought him at least halfway back, to the small city of Cedar Rapids. His early childhood—he was born in 1891 in Jones County near Anamosa—provided the sources for both a critique and a celebration of midwestern life. "His people were Quakers," explained the catalog for his first New York exhibition in 1935,

and he remembers his father returning an unread copy of Grimm's Fairy Tales to a neighbor, thanking him, but saying "We Quakers can read only true things." The boy's first drawing was of his favorite Plymouth Rock hen setting on an impossible number of eggs. "The only drawing materials I could get," he says, "were the large sheets of cheap white cardboard that were enclosed in the wooden boxes of huge square crackers that Father bought in Anamosa. . . . My first studio was underneath the oval dining room table which was covered with a red checkered cloth. The cloth hung with nice arched openings on both sides." Such things as the tangy smell of buffalo robes remembered from winter sleigh rides, the soft patter of summer rain on the low farmhouse roof, and particularly the velvet thrill of the cool earth on his bare feet as he walked across the ploughed fields to school were later to vitalize his portrayals of the scenes and people he knew.[18]

Wood moved to Cedar Rapids with his mother, Hattie, two brothers, Frank and John, and sister Nan after his father died in 1901. He milked neighborhood cows, sold vegetables from Hattie's garden, and delivered drinking water to help support the family. At Washington High School, Wood developed his interest in arts and crafts by painting scenery and drawing for the yearbook and school magazine. He also started an interior decorating business and unpacked paintings for exhibitions put on by the Cedar Rapids Art Association, where he and his friend Marvin Cone would, in Nan's recollection, "spend the early dawn hours copying the Old Masters together."[19]

The summer after graduation Wood went to Minneapolis to study jewelry-making and other handicrafts with Ernest Batchelder at the School of Design and Handicraft and Normal Art, supporting himself for a while by working as a night watchman in a mortuary. Wood's first biographer speculated that by reading Batchelder's magazine *The Craftsman* and studying with him in Minneapolis, Wood "acquired the feeling for Gothic architecture" that would lead him to the house in Eldon. Back in Cedar Rapids, he commuted by train and foot to teach in a one-room schoolhouse, started a jewelry business, and made his way some evenings to Iowa City, where he audited a life-drawing class at the University of Iowa. In 1913, he moved to Chicago to study at the Art Institute. Another jewelry business failed, and unemployed and unable to continue his studies, he returned again to Cedar Rapids. When his mother's mortgage was foreclosed, Grant built her a cabin, where he, Hattie, and Nan lived from 1917 to 1924, when they moved to 5 Turner Alley behind the mortuary.

In 1918, he enlisted in the army and, stationed in Washington, D.C., designed camouflage for cannons; he earned extra money by drawing portraits of his fellow soldiers. The next year he started teaching at Jackson Junior High School in Cedar Rapids and had a two-man exhibition with Marvin Cone at Killian's Department Store. In 1922, he took a job at McKinley Junior High.[20]

Wood and Cone traveled to Paris in the summer of 1920. Wood returned in 1923 to study at the Académie Julien and again in 1926, producing many derivative Impressionist paintings that sold poorly at an exhibition at the Galerie Carmine. What endured from his exposure to late nineteenth-century French painting was the influence of Georges Seurat's pointillism. Commissioned by the American Legion to design and direct the construction of a stained glass window for the Cedar Rapids Veterans Memorial Building, Wood went to Munich in 1928, where he added the influences of Hans Memling and other Flemish and German Renaissance painters. "He liked the crystalline realism of the Flemish artist," Wanda Corn suggests; "it reminded him of the way he himself had worked as a child, before his teachers insisted that his work be soft and evocative." He may also have been exposed to Art Deco and the Neue Sachlichkeit (New Objectivity) movement, though as Corn argues, his appreciation of "their heightened realism" would have been tempered by his disapproval of their Weimar "disgust, cynicism, and social criticism." A disagreement between Wood and the Legion over the wording of the window's inscription—Wood wanted something "simple" and "dignified," according to Nan, whereas the Legion "loudly demanded a long, flowery text"—delayed the window's dedication for twenty-seven years.[21]

Wood had quit public-school teaching in 1927. He now made his living by painting, most lucratively portraits of Cedar Rapids "society" people and their children. His 1929 portrait of his mother, *Woman with Plants*, was his first in the "neo-Flemish" style of "severe poses, intense expressions and hard lines." It was also his first to place his model in front of an Iowa background. Hattie appeared in a rickrack-fringed apron with her cameo, holding a tall potted plant—a sanseveira or "snake plant." Behind her were neatly tied haystacks, a red barn, a windmill, a winding river, rounded trees, rolling fields, and a cloudless sky. Two more paintings in his new style followed before *American Gothic*.[22]

Driving away, I stopped and snapped a photo of the house from the city maintenance building across the road. There were junked cars and a propane tank in the foreground, telephone poles and gravel piles in the middle ground. When I got back home, I called Bruce Thiher, who said that he'd show me the inside of the house on my next trip to Eldon. "I've grown adept at posing people," he wryly boasted. "Bring the wife. We have the costumes and a pitchfork."[23]

By the time I returned in the summer of 2004, Thiher had

moved away. I learned this too late to contact the new care-taker, but I thought I might just knock on the door. I arrived in the evening, to the loud quiet of birds and bugs. Mine was again the only car in the lot, where the sign still promised an education center. The paint on the house was peeling, espe-cially along the verticals above the porch, on the frame of the famous window, the porch posts, and the roof of the extension. The shingles on the porch roof were rotting, but the daffodils around the house were in bloom and the dotted lace curtain in the window looked freshly laundered. A Mountain Dew can lay in the road. I fended off mosquitoes and thought that if I looked through the window from the inside out, I'd have done something that Grant Wood never did. But I'd already visited the house two times to his one, and it didn't look like anyone was home anyway.

With neither the house nor the painting do we really have access to "the real thing," unmediated by overfamiliarity. When we stand where we're supposed to, when we adjust our cameras to duplicate the perspective, when we follow the instructions to see the house as Wood saw it and snap pictures to capture the experience, we are seeking uniqueness and authenticity by repeating and copying. We still won't get to the essential house any more than by staring at the canvas at the Art Institute will we arrive at a true, singular, unchanging *American Gothic*.[24]

"This is a very famous painting," people tell their part-ners, friends, children, parents, husbands, and wives when they come upon *American Gothic* in Gallery 247 at the Art Institute. Usually they get no reply beyond a nod of agree-ment. What can they say? Yes, it is a very famous painting. I am spending the day looking at it, but also looking at other people look at it and eavesdropping on their conversations. I lose count of how many times people say "This is a very famous painting." Parents remind their children, "You've seen this before." A little boy asks his mother, "I saw that, right?" "It's a very famous painting," another mother explains to a child in a stroller. "It's called *American Gothic*. Can you say 'American Gothic'?" "American Gothic," the child answers.

Most people don't speak when they see it. But many of them smile. Because it's so famous? Because they've seen it so many times before, in parodies and advertisements? A tour comes through. The docent observes that lots of visitors ask if this is "the real thing." Maybe they smile because they're imagining, in an unadorned, distressed gilded frame, behind plexiglas, between Diego Rivera's *Portrait of Florence Arquin* and John Steuart Curry's *Hogs Killing a Rattlesnake*, a "real" *American Gothic* that existed before the fame, the parodies, and the advertisements. "Oh, hey, Mom! *American Gothic*!" a man exclaims. "Isn't it funny to actually see it?"

"That was in the movie," a boy—my guess is that he's around ten—points out to his father.

"It's one of *the* most famous American paintings," the father responds. He repeats the observation twice more, with increasing emphasis.

"What movie?" I ask.

"*Ferris Bueller's Day Off*," they reply. I remember that Ferris and his friends visit the Art Institute on their day off from school.

"Can't we take a picture of it?" asks the boy. Lots of visitors photograph the painting, perhaps to remind themselves that they've seen the real thing.

"It's funny, don't you think?" asks the dad.

"No."

"They look very sad and serious, don't they? You've never seen the real painting before. Today you have."[25]

Perhaps it is the ubiquity of the image that makes us want to discover its essence. But from the realization that there is no "original" other than the object that hangs in Gallery 247 comes the possibility of reconnecting *American Gothic* to particular times and places, locating it in a variety of interpretive contexts, seeing it now from different and unfamiliar angles.

Faced with a hostile local reaction to the painting, Wood initially insisted that it was an exercise in composition rather than a comment on anything outside the canvas. Other than a few art historians who have tried to submit *American Gothic* to a purely formalist analysis, nobody has taken Wood at his word. His very first critic—the chairman of the Art Institute's prize committee—assumed by deriding it as a "comic valentine" that it represented particular people and a particular place, and many others soon followed in imagining "real" lives and locales behind or beyond the frame. In 1940, an NBC radio program called "Art for Your Sake" eavesdropped on an imaginary conversation among viewers of the painting:

Voice 1: Here's a painting I can really understand. Boy, has that got a wallop.

Voice 2: That's a *story-telling* picture—a *literary* picture. That's not real art.

Voice 1: I don't know about that, but I do know one thing—that guy in it with the pitchfork sure looks like my Uncle Pete down in Topeka, Kansas.

Voice 3 (Woman, laughing)*:* Yes, and that woman beside him is the very image of our old-maid Cousin Martha up in Vermont.[26]

The realness of the figures alarms a museum guard in a 1961 Charles Addams cartoon. Having climbed down from

The American Gothic *couple leaves the canvas and the museum in Charles Addams's 1961 cartoon. [© Tee and Charles Addams Foundation]*

the painting, they are heading toward him and the museum's exit. My friends overheard an elderly couple's conversation at the Art Institute in 2004:

> *Woman:* Now were they supposed to look angry?
>
> *Man:* No, that's just the way they were born.[27]

How and why did *American Gothic*, its public life perhaps contingent on its narrow rescue from a pile of rejected canvases, become the best known American painting? What does it mean? What has it meant? Were it not for the painting's aesthetic richness, *American Gothic* would not have opened itself up to a variety of interpretive possibilities, to so much cultural work over the years. But *American Gothic*'s meanings don't inhere in the painting. They have emerged from viewers' encounters with it (or with the image much more often than with the painting itself), from the conjunction of what they have brought to it, seen in it, and taken from it. A "storytelling picture," but what stories has it told and to whom?

ICONOCLASM

An Iowa farmwife, irate over *American Gothic*, told Grant Wood, by one account, that he should have his "head bashed in." Wood remembered the threat as only a bit less violent, without the emphatic "in." Another vowed to bite off his ear. "I saw a trim white cottage, with a trim white porch—a cottage built on several Gothic lines," he recalled in a 1933 interview.

> This gave me an idea. That idea was to find two people who, by their severely straight-laced characters, would fit into such a home. I looked about among the folks I

knew around my home town, Cedar Rapids, Iowa, but could find none among the farmers—for the cottage was to be a farmer's home. I finally induced my own maiden sister to pose and had her comb her hair straight down her ears, with a severely plain part in the middle. The next job was to find a man to represent the husband. My quest finally narrowed down to the local dentist, who reluctantly consented to pose. I sent to a Chicago mail order house for the prim, colonial print apron my sister wears and for the trim, spotless overalls the dentist has on. I posed them side by side, with the dentist holding stiffly upright in his right hand a three-tined pitchfork. The trim, white cottage appears over their shoulders in the background.

When the picture was printed in the newspapers, I received a storm of protest from Iowa farm wives because they thought I was caricaturing them. One of them actually threatened, over the telephone, "to come over and smash my head."

American Gothic's indelibility was born in controversy.[28]

Often captioned *An Iowa Farmer and His Wife*, the picture circulated nationwide in late 1930 and early 1931. Improvements in photoengraving technology, especially the rotogravure (rotary engraving) process in which images were corroded with acid into a metal cylinder, had made the reproduction of high-quality pictures fast and cheap for newspapers. The number of Saturday or Sunday papers featuring separate rotogravure sections peaked at eighty in 1930. A six-and-a-half-by-five-inch version of *American Gothic* appeared in the *New York Times'* rotogravure section on November 9, a week before the image made its way back to Iowa, in the *Des Moines Register*'s own rotogravure section, where it provoked the local outcry. Pictures wouldn't be effectively distributed by wire services for another six years. (The Associated Press used airplanes in the 1920s and early 1930s to speed the delivery of photos for important stories.) But a New York outfit called the Dorr News Service did a very efficient job of disseminating *American Gothic* to newspapers by mail. After a first showing in the *Chicago Evening Post* on October 28, it appeared in the *New York Herald Tribune*, *Boston Evening Transcript*, *Boston Herald*, *Kansas City Star*, *Omaha World-Herald*, *Christian Science Monitor*, *Indianapolis Star*, *Cedar Rapids Gazette*, and other papers across the country. The *Boston Post Sunday Magazine* featured an eleven-by-nine version on March 22. Unless they saw it on exhibit or sent a pricey three dollars (about $32 today) to Dorr for their own copy, most people first saw it in black and white. It took four years for a color version to appear in a mass circulation magazine: a full-page reproduction in *Time* in December 1934.[29]

While many Iowans reveled in the success of a native son, others—less threateningly but just as vehemently as the skull-endangering farmwife—denounced *American Gothic* as offensive and Wood as an ingrate. "I thought I might have discovered the 'missing link,'" complained Mrs. Earl Robinson from the town of Collins. "Mr. Wood might have depicted his subjects true to life, but the next time he might choose something wholesome to look at and not such oddities. I advise him to hang this portrait in one of our fine Iowa cheese factories. That woman's face would positively sour milk." Inez Keck of Washta decried the "inordinately 'solemncholy' " looks on the couple's faces and proposed the alternative title of "Return From the

Funeral." Mrs. Keck guessed that Wood hadn't been in Iowa since what must have been his long-past childhood, "for no Iowa couple that I've ever known (and I'm no spring chicken, myself) looks as sad as Wood's painting." Mrs. Ray R. Marsh, also of Washta, exclaimed with a similarly sharp sense of humor, "if this is all our work and progress has brought us (Iowa farmers' wives), we might as well quit the job and take up bootlegging or some other up-to-date job! We at least have progressed beyond the three-tined pitchfork stage!"[30]

The barrage of protests to the Art Institute was so heavy that the museum had to reply by form letters, reported the Omaha paper when the painting appeared there in March 1931. The museum didn't object to such publicity and in its newsletter described how Wood had received a phone call from an "indignant" woman who "used language no lady, Iowan or otherwise should use."[31]

Some, like Mrs. Marsh, objected to the painting's portrayal of "An Iowa *Farmer* and His Wife." *American Gothic* was an insult to farmers, who were hardly the primitives, the pitchfork-wielding missing links, Wood had depicted. Others were most offended by the apparent relationship between the two figures: "An Iowa Farmer and His *Wife*" or, as the *Hammond Times* of Indiana put it (with a Solomon D. Butcher photograph in mind?), "This Nebraska homesteader and his Swedish wife." The man seemed too old to be married to the woman.[32]

Wood immediately responded that he hadn't intended the figures to be farmers. He told the press: "All of this criticism would be good fun if it was made from any other angle. I do not claim the two people painted are farmers. I hate to be misunderstood as I am a loyal Iowan and love my native state. All that I attempted to do was to paint a picture of a Gothic house and to depict the kind of people I fancied should live in that house." The clothing, he explained, indicated that these people were "small-town" rather than country folk. And they were generically small-town. It was "unfair to localize them to Iowa," Wood insisted; they were "American."[33]

Why relocating "those two prim, stern people" from farm to town made much of a difference, Wood didn't reveal, and he later contradicted himself in saying (in 1933, by which time the painting was already being seen differently) that "the cottage was to be a farmer's home." But placing his figures in a small town seemed to mollify the farmwives. Meanwhile, the clever move from Smalltown, Iowa, to Smalltown, U.S.A., probably defused any potential attacks from, say, the residents of Eldon. Wood also tried to ward off criticism by asserting that his primary concern was with form rather than content, aesthetics rather than satire: "It was my intention, later, to do a Mission bungalow painting as a companion piece, with Mission bungalow types standing in front of it. The accent then, of course, would be put on the horizontal instead of the vertical." *American Gothic*, in the art historian James Dennis's characterization of Wood's parry, was more "a play on visual forms" than a play on farmers or townspeople, Iowan or American. Wood never painted *American Mission*.[34]

Who was offended by the idea that the man and woman in the painting were married—and why the age disparity scandalized them—is more of a mystery. Wood's friend and patron Edward Rowan rose to *American Gothic*'s defense a week after it received the Harris prize by observing that "the artist has taken liberties with his sitters but has not resorted to unpleasant distortion" in his depiction of the "simple farm couple." Wood himself didn't comment on the relationship when he responded to the criticism that *American Gothic* ridiculed Iowa farmers, though in the 1933 interview he referred to the man as "the husband." It was Nan who first insisted that her brother intended the figures to be father and daughter, not husband and wife. "I am not supposed to be the gentleman's wife, but his daughter," she insisted in the *Des Moines Register*'s "open forum" about the painting in December 1930. Then she elaborated on the characters:

> I get my ash blond hair from mother's side of the family; papa keeps a feed store—or runs the village post-office, or perhaps he preaches in the little church. . . . Anyhow, he is a very religious person. When he comes home in the evening, our Jersey cow out in the barn starts to moo, and so father takes off his white collar, pulls on overalls and an old coat, and goes out to hay the cow. . . .
>
> I am supposed to be one of those terribly nice and proper girls who get their chief joy in life out of going to Christian Endeavor and frowning horribly at the young couples in back seats if they giggle or whisper.

Maybe Nan, at thirty, was personally troubled by the thought of being married to a sixty-three-year-old man. Though Grant later called her a "maiden" when he explained the origins of the painting, she'd been married since 1924 to Edward Graham, a tubercular "wanderer" (Nan's word) who was living in New Mexico while Nan lived with Grant and Hattie at 5 Turner Alley. The thought still disturbed her enough fourteen years later to revise her brother's contribution to the *Register*'s forum when she quoted it in her reminiscences about Grant.

In her version, Grant answers "the fury of the farmers and their wives" by explaining that

> I simply invented some American Gothic people to stand in front of a house of this type. The people in *American Gothic* are not farmers but small-town people, as the shirt on the man indicates. My sister posed as the woman. She is supposed to be the man's daughter, not his wife. I hate to be misunderstood as I am a loyal Iowan and love my state.

It is possible that Nan restored a line clarifying the couple's relationship that had been edited out of Grant's published statement; it is equally possible that she added her own words and attributed them to her brother.[35]

Gothic," according to the fourth definition in the 1929 edition of *Webster's Collegiate Dictionary*, meant "of, pertaining to, or designating a style of building and ornament"; hence: the window. The first two definitions referred to the historical Goths. The third may account in part for Iowans' angry reaction to the painting: "Of, pertaining to, or characteristic of, the Middle Ages; medieval; derogatorily, of, pertaining to, or characteristic of the Dark Ages; hence: rude; barbarous." The *Collegiate Dictionary* omitted the literary associations of the word, though they were certainly known at the time. The first self-described gothic novel was Horace Walpole's *The Castle of Otranto*, subtitled *A*

Gothic Story (1764). It set the terms for the genre as popularized by Ann Radcliffe, Mary Shelley, Matthew "Monk" Lewis
in England, Charles Brockden Brown, and, of course, Edgar
Allan Poe in the United States: gloom, terror, haunting, possession, degeneration, decay, secrecy, murder, seduction,
incest, tormented souls and tortured bodies, hidden vices and
perversions behind the veneer of virtue.[36]

A State Historical Society of Iowa discussion guide for
school visits to the American Gothic House urges students to
ponder the question, "Why is the woman looking in a different direction than the man?" and offers the suggestion "that
she was embarrassed to have her 'picture' taken." The uncertainty about the figures' relationship, despite Nan's best
efforts to establish them as father and daughter, has invited
all kinds of speculation. The critic John E. Seery raises the
intriguing possibility that the house isn't the only gothic element of the painting. "If the term *gothic* admits of counter-
vailing senses, the reverential *and* the horrifying," writes
Seery, "then much depends on whether and how the couple is
a couple." Could the woman, dwelling in the lonely house in
the cornfields or on the edge of town, be both "wife" and
daughter? Does the pitchfork signify something secret, dark,
satanic? The woman's "apron pattern seems to rhyme with the
pattern of the closed curtains behind the gothic window
upstairs—and so we naturally wonder," Seery contends,
"What goes on behind those closed curtains?"[37]

(A 1988 slasher movie titled *American Gothic* featured the
taglines "Families that slay together stay together!" and "A
picture-perfect camping trip becomes a portrait in terror." The
posters and video box armed the woman with a knife to com-
plement the man's pitchfork. Terrified victims await their

doom behind the gothic window as streaks of lightning strike the house. The fact that one-time A-list actors Rod Steiger and Yvonne DeCarlo starred in the film—and struck the *American Gothic* pose on the promotional materials—sounds an additional gothic note of decay.[38])

Since Grant, more so than Nan, was a "spinster" when he painted *American Gothic*, Seery imagines that the painting is "haunted" by "Oedipal, generational, incestual themes." Wood supposedly told a friend that he wasn't likely to get married while his mother was alive and confessed to another, "I guess I'm just not interested in women." In 1935, he married Sara Maxon, described by Nan as a woman with "a great need or urge to dominate and direct social conversations," and divorced her in 1939, ending what Nan called "a traumatic nightmare." In *American Gothic*, the figure modeled on Nan wears the cameo that Grant gave to Hattie and that she wore, along with a rickrack apron like Nan's in *American Gothic*, in Wood's 1929 painting *Woman with Plants. American Gothic*, says Seery, urges us to ask, "How was a man in the 30s" (or now) "supposed to portray his caring if sexually stultifying relationship to his widowed mother?"[39]

Whether viewers of the painting in the 1930s thought about its "ambiguous sexuality" we can't know. But we do know that the secrets of small-town lives intrigued Wood's contemporaries. In Thomas Wolfe's 1929 bestseller, *Look Homeward, Angel*, his alter ego Eugene Gant mused about the mysteries behind the façades of his North Carolina hometown of "Altamont." "He believed in the infinite rich variety of all the towns and faces: behind any of a million shabby houses he believed there was strange buried life, subtle and shattered romance, something dark and unknown. At the moment of passing any house, he thought, some one therein might be at the gate of death, lovers might lie twisted in hot embrace, murder might be doing." Appearing at a time when repression had become a familiar term to self-styled moderns steeped in popular Freudianism, *American Gothic* invited viewers to contemplate what lay repressed—though perhaps not in such "rich variety" as Gant imagined—behind the painting's surface.[40]

This association of *American Gothic* with repression resurfaced in the cult classic *The Rocky Horror Picture Show* (1975), where the image twice beckons the squeaky-clean small-town couple Brad Majors (Barry Bostwick) and Janet Weiss (Susan Sarandon) into a delightfully gothic world of mad scientists, space aliens, androgyny, transvestism, glam rock, and polymorphous sexuality. In the opening wedding scene, as midnight moviegoers fling rice at the screen, the *American Gothic* pair flanks the doors of the Denton (Ohio) Episcopal Church. They blandly contribute backing vocals to Brad and Janet's duet ("Dammit Janet"), open the church doors for them, and wheel a coffin onto the pulpit as the oblivious young lovers look into each other's eyes and, inspired by their friends' wedding, pledge their engagement. That night they are equally oblivious to Richard Nixon's resignation speech on the car radio when their tire blows out in a rain storm. Seeking refuge in the castle of Frank N. Furter, they are greeted first by the butler Riff Raff and then by the maid Magenta, clearly played by the same actors (Richard O'Brien, who wrote *Rocky Horror*, and Patricia Quinn) who played the *American Gothic* couple in the wedding scene. The painting itself is mounted in the castle's vestibule, next to a clock that is also a coffin. Riff launches into "The Time Warp," the midnight audience sings and dances along, and Brad and

Janet are ushered into the bacchanalia of the Annual Tran-
sylvanian Convention. Still absurdly innocent, Brad remarks
to the terrified Janet, "They're probably foreigners with ways
different from our own." Even after he's had oral sex with
Frank N. Furter (Tim Curry), who assures him that "there's no
crime in giving yourself over to pleasure," Brad wants to
return to the small-town womb. In the climactic orgy, he sings
"It's beyond me/Help me Mommy/I'll be good you'll see/Take
this dream away."[41]

On an apparently more wholesome note, a recent online
sermon titled "You Might Want to Hold Off on the Judging" uses
American Gothic to enter into the text of I Corinthians 4:3–5:

1. I'm sure that most of you have seen Grant Wood's
   famous painting of an old Indiana [sic] couple posing in front of their farmhouse. The painting is
   considered the definitive portrait of the Midwestern farmer and his wife. But the truth is, the people portrayed in the painting were neither farmers
   and they were not a couple. Wood's sister, Nan,
   was the model for the woman and a dentist friend
   named Byron McKeeby posed as the man. And the
   "farmhouse" in the picture was once used as a bordello. (*Uncle John's Ultimate Bathroom Reader*)

2. The painting reminds us that things are not
   always what they seem. When it comes to passing
   judgment, it is best to hold off, for things are not
   always what they seem. Furthermore, judgment
   should be reserved for a later time and reserved
   for someone that is better qualified.

Nan would have been pleased that some people, at least, are still willing to defer to her expertise on the couple's relationship. *Uncle John's Ultimate Bathroom Reader*, however, turns out not to be a reliable source; the house was never a bordello. The gothic interpretations of the painting are even more impassioned than the sermon in asserting that "things are not always what they seem."[42]

Critics who admired *American Gothic* in the early 1930s agreed with those who loathed it that the painting was a satire. It lampooned American rural or small-town life, its rigidity and provincialism, its repressed and oppressive people, pinched, puritanical Bible-thumpers, fundamentalists, according to the label popularized by the 1925 Scopes "Monkey" Trial in Dayton, Tennessee (thus Mrs. Robinson's invocation of the missing link), nativists, Ku Kluxers perhaps, powerful atavisms in a society that the census had proclaimed predominantly urban in 1920. The "thin-lipped, leathery faced" farmer and his wife, "two extremely prim and proper, thoroughly righteous persons," "unsmiling and evidently taking life very seriously," were "solidly grounded on Puritan principles." In light of the confusion over the painting's name—its widespread mislabeling as *An Iowa Farmer and His Wife*—critics suggested as alternatives *Immaculate Primness* and *Puritan Happiness*.[43]

The obscurity of the artist who had produced such a sensational image encouraged the critic Walter Prichard Eaton to create a scenario behind the "grim-visaged" figures. ("Grim-visaged" was a favorite description among the painting's admirers.) Wood, wrote Eaton, had discovered "fertile" ground for American artists. "Let them go in for social satire." Though Eaton knew "nothing of the artist and his history,"

> we cannot help believing that as a youth he suffered tortures from these people, who could not understand the joy of art within him and tried to crush his soul with their sheet iron brand of salvation. They are rather terrible. The longer you look at them, the more you realize they might come from many parts of this country—but from no other.

American Gothic, in Eaton's view, was about the hostility of its subjects toward their very presence in the painting; the man is glaring and the woman is looking away because they hate art and artists. A prominent drama critic, occasional playwright, supporter of the Little Theater movement, and later a professor at the Yale School of Fine Arts, Eaton saw art as triply besieged by Puritanism, mass ignorance, and commercialism. "When exploiters flourish," he declared, "art pines." He was especially disdainful of the movies, which appealed to "the great common denominator of the American population, with 35 to 40 year old bodies and minds 11 to 12 years old." Grant Wood, whoever he was, had in *American Gothic* simultaneously captured and defied those who would "crush" artistic expression.[44]

The most influential endorsement of the painting came from Christopher Morley, who like Eaton undertook the mission of combating America's Philistines by promoting the cause of art. An important arbiter of middlebrow culture in his

Saturday Review of Literature column, "The Bowling Green," and from his seat on the Selecting Committee of the Book-of-the-Month Club, Morley told his readers that "the time to patronize art is while it is alive and kicking. If I were able to buy pictures one kind of artist whose work I should want to buy would be Grant Wood of Cedar Rapids, Iowa. Some weeks ago I saw, in the rotogravure section of the New York *Times*, a photo of his gorgeous painting 'American Gothic.'" Like Eaton, Morley ventured behind the seemingly transparent picture plane to speculate about the "lives" of the people Wood depicted. "In those sad yet fanatical faces" he could "read much both of what is Right and what is Wrong with America." What was right was the tenacity and integrity of both the figures and the artist who painted them despite the figures' animosity toward creativity and culture; what was wrong was this animosity—their fanatical and cramped religiosity. "The man's sombre eyes, tight lips, and knuckled hand on the pitchfork" reminded him of Oliver Cromwell. As Joan Shelley Rubin has noted, Morley's conception of art as a spiritual realm ideally untainted by commerce didn't preclude a marketer's savvy for promoting art and literature that he admired. His column on *American Gothic*—"one of the most thrilling American paintings I had ever seen," in his hucksterish phrase—included the recommendation that his readers buy prints of it; he conveniently included the price and address for ordering them, along with the assurance that "doing so will be doing more to encourage art than . . . importing a wagonload of Murillos."[45]

Even if we could know for certain what Wood intended *American Gothic* to be about—and we can't—the painting's meanings have much more to do with viewers' perceptions than with his intentions. And many viewers over the years, starting with Eaton and Morley, have perceived *American Gothic* as satire. No less an authority on modern art than Gertrude Stein, whose opinions the American press eagerly reported in the 1930s, praised Wood as "the foremost American painter" and declared, "We should fear Grant Wood. Every artist and every school of artists should be afraid of him, for his devastating satire." Stein just missed an opportunity to see if Wood was as frightening in person as he was on canvas. In 1934, he and some colleagues at the University of Iowa organized a lecture series under the auspices of a club they called The Society for the Prevention of Cruelty to Speakers. The S.P.C.S. entertained its visitors—Christopher Morley was the first—in a couple of rooms above Smitty's Café in Iowa City, furnished in what Wood described as "the worst style of the late Victorian period," including Currier and Ives prints and "God Bless Our Home," "Peace Be With You," and "Home Sweet Home" embroideries. By reconstituting itself as "A Rose Is A Rose Club" and sending Stein a picture of themselves wearing white roses, the members of the S.P.C.S. persuaded her to be their guest during her American lecture tour. The eager audience that trudged through a sleet storm to see her on the evening of December 10, 1934, went home disappointed. Stein's plane was grounded in Waukesha, Wisconsin, and the self-described genius, friend and patron of Picasso and Matisse, never met her favorite American satirist.[46]

Critics, curiously grounding their interpretations in confident assertions about Wood's intentions, continued into the 1940s and beyond to debate the satire issue. H. W. Janson emphatically claimed in 1946 that *American Gothic* "had been intended as a satire on small-town American life." Matthew Baigell ascribed the same satiric intent to the painting in 1974 when he insisted that the figures "exude a generalized, barely repressed animosity that borders on venom" and symbolize "the malevolent spirits that inhabited this region." In 1983, Wanda Corn challenged what she saw as "the conventional historical wisdom" emanating from Eaton through Janson, Baigell, and others, and sought to refute "the notion that Wood intended to satirize his couple-with-pitchfork."[47]

With characteristic assurance, Robert Hughes told the viewers and readers of his *American Visions* in 1997 the reason why Wood and his mass audience couldn't decide whether or not the painting was satirical: "Wood was a timid and deeply closeted homosexual," and *American Gothic*, rather than offering up a forceful, unambiguous, straight, or uncloseted satire, was "an exercise in sly camp, the expression of a gay sensibility so cautious that it can hardly bring itself to mock its objects openly." John Seery tried to mediate the issue a year later by contending that "*satire* isn't quite the right word" for what Wood was up to in the painting; Wood, he maintained, was an ironist, committed to a "juggling of heterogeneous if not contradictory perspectives," playfully inviting open, participatory, democratic interpretation of his work. (Seery pointed out the tautology of Hughes's explanation: Wood's timid, closeted homosexuality accounts for the painting's sly camp, which expresses a cautious gay sensibility, which indicates that Wood was a timid, closeted homosexual.) We can see the artist's deliberate elusiveness, according to Seery, in his comment about *American Gothic* that "there is satire in it but only as there is satire in any realistic statement":

These are types of people I have known all my life. I tried to characterize them truthfully—to make them more like themselves than they were in actual life. They had their bad points, and I did not paint these under, but to me they were basically good and solid people. I had no intention of holding them up to ridicule.

Even if an artist's unambiguous statements of his intentions can establish what a painting *really* means, Wood gave so many contradictory accounts of *American Gothic*, deliberately or not, that the question of whether it is in essence satirical, fortunately, can't ever be settled.[48]

The story," Wood "cryptically" told an interviewer in 1940, "begins with Mencken."[49]

The reference may have been cryptic by the time of *American Gothic*'s tenth anniversary, but in 1930 it would have been surprising had an aspiring American artist *not* claimed the influence of H. L. Mencken. Mencken was a culture hero in America's bohemias and among "moderns" in the 1920s, admired not so much for his cynicism as for his "ironic cultural nationalism" (the phrase is the literary critic George Hutchinson's)—his appeal to creative and intellectual independence against stifling conformity and false values, whether in the "Bible Belt" (Mencken coined the term) or among "the so-called fashionable folk of the large cities—chiefly wealthy industrials in the interior-decorator and country-club stage of culture." F. Scott Fitzgerald, who received Mencken's crucial support early in his literary career, divulged in 1920 that he and his friend, the fledgling critic Edmund Wilson, were thoroughly "saturated with Menckenia." Though reading Mencken itself became quite fashionable, the badge of sophistication and cultural superiority that saturation in Menckenia conferred probably figured less significantly to a young painter in Iowa (and to Fitzgerald and Wilson, for that matter) than did his earnest summons for "autonomous, curious, venturesome, courageous" literature and art.[50]

Mencken's attacks on the Midwest were only slightly less malicious than his famous indictment of the South in "The Sahara of the Bozart," originally published in 1920. That "gargantuan paradise of the fourth rate," he complained of the former confederacy, "is almost as sterile, artistically, intellectually, culturally, as the Sahara desert." Whether in agreement or reaction, Southern writers rose to meet Mencken's challenge by producing their own critical assessments of the region and by creating work that would reveal the South's cultural fertility.[51]

Walter Prichard Eaton's perception of *American Gothic* as a defense of art against the "sheet iron brand of salvation" dovetailed with Mencken's equation in "The Sahara of the Bozart" and elsewhere of Philistinism and Puritanism as the twin blights of American civilization. The Philistine's benighted sense of "human life, not as an agreeable adventure, but as a mere trial of rectitude and efficiency," and "the Puritan's utter lack of aesthetic sense, his distrust of all romantic emotion, his unmatchable intolerance of opposition, his unbreakable belief in his own bleak and narrow views, his savage cruelty of attack, his lust for relentless and barbarous persecution," manifested themselves in the 1920s, to Mencken's amusement and disgust, in Prohibition and the Scopes Trial. This assault on Puritanism and Philistinism extended well beyond Mencken; it figured centrally in American artistic and intellectual life in the 1910s and 1920s—in, for example, Harold Stearns's famous 1922 symposium *Civilization in the United States*, to which Mencken contributed an essay on politics. All the contributors agreed, Stearns wrote, that "the most moving and pathetic fact in the social life of America to-day is emotional and aesthetic starvation." The Puritan and the Philistine combined with a third, usually interchangeable type—the materialistic, anti-artistic, anti-intellectual "Pioneer"—to serve as "the cultural villains of the era," in the historian Warren Susman's phrase: emblems of a "useless past" invoked to counter "what was considered to be the Midwestern domination of American life and values."[52]

Anti-Philistinism and anti-Puritanism were the guiding themes of bohemias across the country in the 1910s and 1920s—Greenwich Village, most famously, but also many local variants. By the mid-1920s, novels and memoirs were recalling the pre–World War I Iowa bohemia that preceded Wood's: the Davenport writers' colony of Floyd Dell, George Cram "Jig" Cook, and Susan Glaspell. "We were the queer fish of the town," Glaspell remembered; "get the queer fish in town into one pond and it's a queer pond—but it moves the water around." Gathering first at the home of the radical Rabbi William Fineshriber, then above a saloon as a club of "freethinkers" they called the Monist Society, the Davenport bohemians felt at first, in Dell's words, that the town's extraordinary literary and intellectual life "was a special miracle performed by a suddenly kind universe" and only later recognized the "definite social forces" behind it: "German and Jewish, with an 1848 European revolutionary foundation, and a liberal and Socialist superstructure." Before they moved on to other bohemias in the 1910s—Chicago, Greenwich Village, Provincetown—and to artistic success—Dell as critic and novelist, Glaspell as novelist and playwright, Cook as playwright and founder of the Provincetown Players—they fashioned in Davenport new, liberated selves. "Me, skeptic, vagabond, rebel and infidel," wrote Dell in a Davenport poem, his self-characterization closely prefiguring Mencken's conception of the artist as "autonomous, curious, venturesome, courageous." Cook even imagined Iowa farmers freed from Puritanism, Philistinism, and Pioneering—from "mindless toil," "unlaboring ease," and "crusted superstition":

Here

Avoid both half-lives of this sordid age—
The slavish drudgery of mindless toil—
The sleek stagnation of unlaboring ease.
Loving the wondrous earth, let equal hand
And brain revive the ancient pastoral charm
Of Roman field and vineyard. Iowa
Means soil as flourishing and life as sane
And skies as exquisite and stars as high
And richer-natured people when at last
The morning light of nature-knowledge strikes
Their frigid glass and thaws the settled frost
Of crusted superstition from their souls.[53]

Wood may have been a milder bohemian than these Davenport rebels, but he was a bohemian nonetheless. Cedar Rapids, though it lacked the revolutionary foundation and liberal-socialist superstructure of Davenport, had its share of

dissenters. One was William L. Shirer, a hometown friend of
Wood who became a foreign correspondent famous for his
reporting on World War II. Shirer recalled his return to Cedar
Rapids after a summer working with Wobblies (members of
the radical Industrial Workers of the World) in the western
Nebraska wheatfields. The "tramps" of the I.W.W. had shown
him "that you didn't have to live conventionally, settle down,
get a steady job, get married and have children, join a church,
a lodge, Rotary or Kiwanis, and all that, to fulfill yourself."
Shirer knew that "such thoughts" were "bound to sound subversive if expressed in the churchy, Republican, wholesome-
family atmosphere of Cedar Rapids."[54]

Another was Carl Van Vechten, whom Wood probably
never met though he must have been aware of him. Born
eleven years before Wood, Van Vechten grew up in Cedar
Rapids in the 1880s and 1890s before moving on to Chicago
and New York and a career as novelist, critic, photographer,
friend of modernists from Gertrude Stein to Langston Hughes,
H. L. Mencken to George Gershwin, and patron of the Harlem
Renaissance. Shirer called him a "sort of invisible force,
especially for the young and rebellious in our town." When
Van Vechten, after the publication of his novel *The Tattooed
Countess*, paid a return visit to his hometown in 1924, he
advised Shirer, "off the record," "to get the hell out of Cedar
Rapids as quickly as possible."[55]

The Tattooed Countess is set in the Iowa town of "Maple
Valley"—a thinly disguised Cedar Rapids described by the
hero, seventeen-year-old Gareth Johns, as a "dull, sordid village" mired in "superstitions, conventions" and "moral idio-
cies" where he feels "imprisoned." The town gossips call him
a "sissy" for spending his time reading and studying; "small-

town minds" can't imagine "that any boy should not grow up with the ideal of becoming a retail boot and shoe merchant"; his father wants to knock "some manliness" into the boy. Gareth loves birds, he explains to Miss Colman, the spinster high school teacher who is in love with him, because "they migrate." He wonders aloud to her about something that would have resonated with Grant Wood: "Nobody ever paints or writes about Iowa. Why not, do you suppose?" We don't learn if Gareth will give vision or voice to his birthplace. He runs off with the Countess Nattatorrini, née Ella Poole of Maple Valley, who has briefly returned to recover from a love affair and who immediately rebels against her hometown's stifling "regard for surfaces," the hypocrisy of its "humdrum existence." "I am tattooed on my arm," the Countess declares in a moment of gothic revelation, "while they are tattooed on their hearts."[56]

Wood's Cedar Rapids bohemia emanated from Turner Alley, which by 1926 he envisioned as an artists' colony—the city's "Latin Quarter," as the local newspaper delighted in calling it; the "Greenwich Village of the Corn Belt," Wood supposedly boasted, "the only truly Bohemian atmosphere west of Hoboken." After the farmwives' outcry over *American Gothic*, his friend MacKinlay Kantor described Wood and Turner Alley for the readers of his column in the *Des Moines Tribune-Capital*:

> His attic apartment is crammed with quaint bits of pottery, bronzes, etchings and curios . . . And an undertaker keeps his hearses downstairs . . . Grant Wood is a bachelor, and lives with a quiet, sweet faced woman who is his mother . . . He has a disappearing

cupboard, disappearing dining table and disappearing bed. Everything but the bathtub is apt to disap-
pear at a moment's notice . . . Pink of face and plump
of figure, Iowa's most famous artist calls forth the
mental adjectives "cherubic," "seraphic" and all
the rest. Perhaps he was most nearly in character one
night when he appeared at a costume party dressed as
an angel—wings, pink flannel nightie, pink toes and
even a halo supported by a stick thrusting up from his
back . . .

(Kantor went on to write the novel on which the Oscar-winning
movie *The Best Years of Our Lives* was based, the story and
screenplay for the noir classic *Gun Crazy*, and the Pulitzer
Prize–winning Civil War epic *Andersonville*.)[57]

David Turner, Wood's undertaker friend and patron,
donated an old mortuary building for him "to fix up as a studio
and teaching place for artists, a sort of Studio House" for
musicians, painters, and writers. "Studio House was not a
Bohemian outfit," one of its residents, Hazel Brown, later proclaimed. She meant that they weren't poseurs and dilet-
tantes—but then neither were most of the bohemians of
Davenport or Greenwich Village. "The artists," Brown wrote,
"were serious young people who wanted a 'home'—a place to
work, teach, and study together. They were all capable of
earning their living from their talents if given an opportunity."
Turner Alley soon became the site of a community theater,
along with lots of parties, though Wood assured the local press
that this artists' colony would not "reach the lurid heights" of
other bohemias. After all, his "quiet, sweet faced" mother

lived in Turner Alley too. Studio House "remained a lively place for several years," according to Nan, until Turner, pressed during the Depression to keep up on its taxes, had to have it knocked down.[58]

Edward Rowan didn't share Mencken's idea of the Midwest as a vast cultural wasteland, but it isn't a stretch to think of his experiment in fine arts as a response, not unlike that of Southern writers, to Mencken's challenge. The Little Gallery, launched two years after Studio House and, with its Carnegie money, on much more solid footing, featured both traveling exhibitions and shows of local artists' work, including Wood's. "There is certainly no need for the corn belt to hide hands that are hard from the struggle with the soil," the *Des Moines Register* commented in celebrating the efforts of Rowan and the Little Gallery in Cedar Rapids. "But neither can it afford to shun the enterprises aiming at cultural advancement." These efforts—along with the "national recognition of Grant Wood's work" that they helped nurture— had successfully contested the "popular conception elsewhere in the country that the drabness of the corn belt was far from conducive to the development of artistic talent." Jay Sigmund, a Cedar Rapids insurance executive and poet, confessed to Rowan that before the creation of the Little Gallery, he would "often get in a spiritual doldrum" and find himself "yearning for some of the things which big cities afforded and which our own smaller town lacked." The Little Gallery lifted him from those "most depressing" times, "marked a new epoch" in his life and, by "awakening our consciousness in the Middle West," in the cultural life of the city and region. Rowan himself, usually modest and mild-mannered, adopted Mencken's rhetoric in describing his Cedar Rapids sojourn.

To "create an art consciousness in his community, county and state," one

> must be a veritable paragon of wisdom and virtue, not only an authority on the history of art but a psychiatrist as well, endowed with a never failing love of humanity, the sensitivity of a poet, the patience of a Job, the arduous zeal of a Jesuit, the diplomacy of a Disraeli, the salesmanship of a Semite and the proverbial indefatigability of an American Indian.[59]

As an established and popular artist in the later 1930s and early 1940s, Wood looked back on his Mencken discipleship with regret and suggested that his mature work—starting with *Woman with Plants* and *American Gothic*—derived from the *repudiation* of Mencken and similar cosmopolitan critics of small-town and rural life. By his own account, he delighted—"ate it up"—as "good old Mencken belabored my people as 'corn-fed boobs and peasants'" in the pages of the *Smart Set* and the *American Mercury*. He fled to Paris to "get clean away from the boobish taboos of the uncultured Bible belt," explained a profile of the artist as a mature man. But then he dug in. "I shall adjust myself to the home town of Cedar Rapids and try to get along," another profile imagined Wood thinking. He returned from his third trip to France, he recalled, "to see, like a revelation, my neighbors in Cedar Rapids, their clothes, their homes, the patterns on their tablecloths and curtains, the tools they use. I suddenly saw all this commonplace stuff as material for art. Wonderful material!" Only by purging himself of "Mencken prejudices" (Mencken's collected essays were published in the twenties in a series of books titled *Prejudices*) did he turn with relish to the authentic subject matter and idiom of his native soil. He became, the profiles insisted, the anti-Mencken: a "Bible Belt Booster."[60]

But if Wood retrospectively characterized *American Gothic* as a move away from Mencken, its initial reception was saturated in the discourse of Menckenism—in Mrs. Robinson's Scopes Trial–inflected reference to the missing link, in Morley's allusion to the Ur Puritan Oliver Cromwell, even in Nan's description of her character as a woman who gets her "chief joy in life out of going to Christian Endeavor." *American Gothic* appeared to its first viewers as the visual equivalent of the revolt-against-the-provinces genre in 1910s and 1920s American literature—the genre, broadly speaking, of Sherwood Anderson's *Winesburg, Ohio* (1919), Dell's *Moon-Calf* (1920), Sinclair Lewis's *Main Street* (1920) and *Babbitt* (1922), as well as Van Vechten's *The Tattooed Countess* and many other novels and short stories. The painting, like the fiction (and like Mencken's criticism), seemed to side with the city against the country and small town, iconoclasm against myth, new against old. No matter that the particular novels and stories often conveyed greater ambivalence than the generic characterization suggested. The Iowa writer Ruth Suckow, for example, whose stories appeared with Mencken's praise in the *Smart Set* and the *American Mercury*, described both the lifelessness of small towns and the urgent "longing for home" of characters who had fled these "rundown, miserable" places. In a nonfiction piece on Iowa in the *Mercury*, Suckow denounced "the Main Street element of small town hardness, dreariness and tense material ambition," along with "the retired farmer element in the towns: narrow, cautious, steady, and thrifty, suspicious of 'culture' but faithful to the churches." But she found hope in "the working farmers": "[r]aw, book-ignorant, travel-ignorant, stubborn and hard-headed; but in their best aspect hard-working, serious-minded, strong and fresh." Another Iowa writer, Herbert Quick, noted the "sources of light" he'd found in the villages and towns of his youth—"souls who led me outward and upward." The presence of these souls, he thought, should temper the prevalent accounts of the towns' "sordid drabness, their utter poverty of inspiration, their lack of men and women above the plane of two-legged horses and cattle."[61]

In 1932, Arthur Millier, the same critic who would celebrate Wood as the "Bible Belt Booster" eight years later, explicitly linked *American Gothic* to contemporary literature in its admirably unflattering realism. "[I]n the patterns of the farmwife's apron and the striping of the man's shirt, the batting of the house, the roof pitch, no less than in the facial lines and expressions," Millier wrote, Wood "was face to face with something real—with such material, in other words, as a good novelist would use. . . . As in the case of a novel, the portrayed are probably the only people who resent it—it is too convincing!" Grant, according to Nan, felt that of all the critics, Millier "had the best understanding of the painting." Neither Grant nor Nan expressed concern in this instance that the critic referred to her character as a "farmwife."[62]

Wood initially described his return to Iowa, his embrace of "native" materials for his art, as a move wholly compatible with the literary projects of the so-called "debunkers" of the 1920s. "I'm going home for good," Shirer remembered him announcing in Paris.

And I'm going to paint those damn cows and barns and barnyards and cornfields and little red school-houses and all those pinched faces and the women in their aprons and the men in their overalls and store suits and the look of a field or a street in the heat of summer or when it's ten below and the snow piled six feet high. Damn it, isn't that what Sinclair Lewis has done in his writing—in *Main Street* and *Babbitt*? Damn it, you can do it in painting, too![63]

Lewis—given a "hearty welcome" by Mencken, whom he idolized, when *Main Street* appeared—was hardly an uncritical celebrant of the Midwest. To portray, in the Lewis mode, the "pinched faces" of "women in their aprons" and "men in their overalls and store suits" was simultaneously and ambivalently to embrace and satirize small-town life. Walter Prichard Eaton even suggested that Lewis ought to buy *American Gothic* with some of his Nobel Prize money, and the *Kansas City Star* soon proclaimed that Wood's popularity was "as great, almost, as the vogue achieved by Sinclair Lewis's 'Main Street' a dozen years ago."[64]

Carol Kennicott, *Main Street*'s heroine, thinks that the town of Gopher Prairie, Minnesota, where she finds herself trapped in her marriage to a local doctor, "where every house was open to view, where every person was but too easy to meet," is too flat and too transparent to conceal anything. And the novel tends to agree with her. Other than Carol, it grants no characters inner lives, and even though it hints at hypocrisies and secrets—at "the shadows of dead thoughts and haunting repressions"—it gives us no alternative to Carol's conception of the town and the townspeople as sluggish, complacent, "savorless," "thoughtless," wholly ruled "by the desire to be respectable"; they are "negation canonized as the one positive virtue," one-dimensional in characterization because they are depthless in essence. Only once does Carol admit to the richness of lives other than her own, when she fleetingly senses that her own narrative has excluded that of her husband: "It has not occurred to her that there was also a story of Will Kennicott, into which she entered only so much as he entered into hers; that he had bewilderments and concealments as intricate as her own, and soft treacherous desires for sympathy."[65]

Main Street locates its "typical" small town at a particular historical moment when Puritanism meets standardization and the combination produces a kind of imperialist provincialism. The novel's narrator, speaking directly through Carol at this point, argues that "a village in a country which is taking pains to become altogether standardized and pure, which aspires to succeed Victorian England as the chief mediocrity of the world, is no longer merely provincial, no longer downy and restful in its leaf-shadowed ignorance. It is a force seeking to dominate the earth. . . ." Reversing the trope of eastern and urban supremacy, *Main Street* imagines a nation under the powerful sway of indistinguishable midwestern towns. From Mencken, Theodore Dreiser, Sherwood Anderson, and other "subversive" writers, Carol learns that "the more intelligent young people . . . flee to the cities with agility and, despite the fictional tradition, resolutely stay there, seldom returning even for holidays." Contrary to the frontier myth, freedom means turning back toward the Atlantic. "Young man, go East," Carol urges Erik Valborg, a tailor's apprentice in Gopher Prairie with artistic aspirations, and her own brief escape from the "grim and old and spying and censorious" town is to the World War I Washington, D.C., of reformers, suffragists, and working women.[66]

In 1936, Wood illustrated a special edition of *Main Street* with a panoply of Gopher Prairie's (or Cedar Rapids') "types"—"The Good Influence," "The Booster," "The Sentimental Yearner," "The Radical," and others. In "The Perfectionist," his drawing of Carol, Wood deftly captured Lewis's characterization of a small-town rebel whose rebellion is itself hopelessly compromised by provincialism—who wages war on Philistinism, as Mencken remarked in his review of *Main Street*, "with essentially Philistine weapons." Carol's "dream of converting a Minnesota prairie town into a sort of Long Island suburb, with overtones of Greenwich Village and the Harvard campus," Mencken sneered, is "absurd." Wood's Carol gazes out at Main Street with an expression of smugness, condescension, and dogmatism; he reveals the irony of her perfectionism—her Puritan-Philistine lack of self-criticism— by making her fail to see that her dress isn't completely buttoned. As Lewis did in *Main Street*, Wood explained that in *American Gothic*, he "endeavored to paint types, not individuals"—or, as a critic astutely put it in 1930, "a composite portrait of all the Uncle Jonathan Wesleys and Aunt Prudence Abigails" (Uncle Whittier and Aunt Bessie Smail in *Main Street*) "of the midwest Bible belt."[67]

Long after his supposed repudiation of Mencken, Wood remained enamored of Lewis and *Main Street*. "I got a great kick out of trying to catch the essence of that story we all admire," he told Lewis after Lewis conveyed admiration for Wood's *Main Street* illustrations. The two men visited each other several times in the late 1930s, and in 1939, asked as a "prominent American" by a Boston newspaper to contribute to its "What Thinking People Read" feature, Wood listed *Main Street* among the five books that had "strongly affected" his ideas. (The others were John Steinbeck's *The Grapes of Wrath*, Erich Maria Remarque's *All Quiet on the Western Front*, John Dos Passos's *Manhattan Transfer*, and *The Autobiography of Lincoln Steffens*.)[68]

Main Street, it turned out, was quite capable of welcoming the popular success of *American Gothic* in the same (or apparently the same) booster spirit that Lewis mocked in his novels. Edward Rowan—in a Rotary Club newspaper!—invited the people of Cedar Rapids to "take pride in Grant Wood's success." Their community, "more than any other in Iowa," had "encouraged its own artists by believing in them to the extent of investing in their paintings." From its inception, the Little Gallery enlisted boosterism in the cause of art. The Kiwanis Club, because it was "both important and interesting" to know what the gallery was doing, decided to hold its meetings there, and the newsletter of the Cedar Rapids Savings Bank noted that if other "typical, normal" American cities followed Cedar Rapids' lead in fostering art appreciation, the nation could prevent the tragedies of starving, suffering, unrecognized artists. "Why I used to think anyone who visited art galleries was a sissy," funeral director David Turner was reported to have said. "Now I never miss an opportunity to visit them"; the Little Gallery got him and others in town "pepped up" for art.

This was the language of Will Kennicott and George Babbitt, twisted around to boost rather than denigrate Main Street's cultural aspirations, in a way that Carol Kennicott could only dream about. *American Gothic* was brought home from Chicago in February 1931 to be displayed at a reception to honor Wood at the Little Gallery, an event that prompted Mrs. S. V. Shouka to thank Rowan for educating Cedar Rapids in the "field of loveliness and beauty" and making possible the triumph of Wood, "the hero of the evening." Mencken and Lewis might have laughed off this celebration as merely another example of Philistinism. But they could just as well have seen it as a rise to the challenge they set out for the Midwest. There, in the Little Gallery, the art boosters of Cedar Rapids looked back into the faces in Wood's painting and proclaimed a victory for the "loveliness and beauty" that Uncle Jonathan/Whittier and Aunt Prudence/Bessie tried to thwart.[69]

One likely point of agreement between viewers of *American Gothic* then and now would be that the people in the painting aren't having any fun, though it's less likely that we'd agree about what kind of fun they aren't having and, more significantly, about the consequence of fun-shunning people among us. When handsome twenty-somethings pose à la *American Gothic* for a Saks Fifth Avenue ad—with ribbed turtlenecks replacing rickrack and overalls, designer rectangular frames substituting for wire rims, and a paint roller (poised for interior decorating) supplanting the pitchfork—we don't really need the tag line "go ahead, live a little" to tell us how anachronistic it would be to exist outside a consumer culture. In 1930 too, the man and woman seemed anachronistic, but because an all-pervasive consumer culture

How far can a parody get away from the original image and still invoke it? American Gothic *sells Saks Fifth Avenue and twenty-something lifestyles. [Grace Huang/Saks Fifth Avenue]*

wasn't yet inevitable, their "grim-visaged" presence was more immediate and their challenge to fun more menacing.

It wasn't only self-styled bohemians, of course, who thought of themselves as modern in the 1920s. By the end of the decade, almost half the people in the United States lived within a thirty-minute drive of a city of 100,000 or more.

Radio, movies, and other nationally distributed forms of entertainment made the identification with the urban and the modern increasingly possible even for people who didn't live in
cities. White-collar work expanded more than any other kind
of employment between 1920 and 1930, and with this expan-
sion came more expendable income and leisure time. Artists
and intellectuals weren't the only ones challenging lingering
Puritanism and Victorianism. So were advertisers, who encouraged middle-class Americans to resist the older values of thrift
and self-denial and to embrace the modern world of leisure and
mass consumption. "Youth," as they were usually labeled in
the period, especially "reveled in modernity," writes the historian Lynn Dumenil. "They viewed their own time as a demar-
cation, a release from the restraints, especially the Victorian
moral code, of the past." And their sense of themselves as modern seemed all the more daring in the face of concerted resist-
ance from the defenders of traditional ways.[70]

In their famous 1929 study of Muncie, Indiana—dubbed
"Middletown" to preserve Muncie's anonymity while establish-
ing that the city under discussion belonged to "that common-
denominator of America, the Middle West"—Robert and Helen
Lynd explained what those couples in back seats were doing
to earn the disapproval of Nan's terribly nice and proper girl:

> There is a small group of girls in the high school who
> are known not to allow "petting." These girls are often
> "respected and popular" but have less "dates"; the
> larger group, "many of them from the 'best families,'"
> with whom "petting parties" are not taboo, are said to
> be much more frequently in demand for movies,
> dances, or automobile parties. Stimulated in part,

probably, by the constant public watching of love-making on the screen, and in part, perhaps, by the sense of safety in numbers, the earlier especially heavy ban upon love-making in public is being relaxed by the young.

Middletown brilliantly explored the tensions, often between generations, produced by the maturing consumer culture and its attendant shift in values, which provoked authorities such as the president of Colgate University to worry about the "danger that leisure, coupled with the comfort and ease of our modern life, will result in both physical and mental degeneracy." One apparently typical "healthy seventeen-year-old high school girl," the Lynds reported, went to the movies twice a week, stayed home only one night in seven, and regularly read a variety of popular magazines, including *Snappy Stories*, *Cosmopolitan*, and *True Story*: "She and her parents are at loggerheads most often, she says, about the way she dresses, and after that, about her use of the family Ford and about her boy and girl friends." Viewers would soon see the same clash of values in *American Gothic*, another "study" of the Midwest.[71]

The denizens of Gopher Prairie in *Main Street* have enthusiastically incorporated elements of the consumer culture—especially movies and "flivvers" (the Ford Model T)—into their lives while continuing to regard genuine pleasure as immoral. These standardized products only reinforce their intolerance, their insistence on conformity, their lack of imagination, what Lewis's narrator described as their "prohibition of happiness," their "slavery self-taught and self-defended," their "dullness made God." Maybe the man in *American Gothic* drove his own flivver. Maybe the woman went to the movies when she wasn't at Christian Endeavor. After all, these were the fruits of America's business civilization. But they could easily abet indecency, and the guardians of purity and propriety had to maintain their vigilance.[72]

Wood dealt more explicitly with anachronism in his 1931 painting *Victorian Survival*, which juxtaposes his austere Aunt Tillie (he based his portrait on an old tintype family photograph) with a modern dial telephone. "There is no way, the artist suggests, for the prim Victorian world of the woman, closed to outsiders and expressions of emotion, to adjust to the jangling, intrusive world of the telephone," writes critic Wanda Corn. "They are creatures from two completely different social systems; the phone is the victor, Aunt Tillie the victim." But modernity's victory didn't seem so certain in *American Gothic*, where the Victorians/Puritans were hardly victims. At a time when commentators such as the journalist and popular historian Frederick Lewis Allen proclaimed a "revolution in manners and morals"—when, according to Allen's 1931 bestseller *Only Yesterday: An Informal History of the Nineteen-Twenties*, "cries of alarm from parents, teachers, and moral preceptors began to rend the air"—the culture war between Victorians/Puritans and moderns remained very much alive, and the moderns enlisted *American Gothic* on their side.[73]

Contemporary viewers saw in the painting an indigenous anti-Puritanism and anti-Philistinism, a native anti-nativism, a cosmopolitan critique of provincialism, a modern send-up of repression that came from direct knowledge and authentic experience. If, as Wood said, they missed its affection, they certainly noticed its sense of humor. Some observed in those faces and in that setting a defense of new forms of leisure and popular culture against a retrograde Victorianism. Some observed new possibilities for American art and culture: vernacular forms and subjects that would be at once authentically American and oppositional, that would counter both provincialism and jingoistic nationalism with cultural nationalism, and that would imagine this alternative nationalism as tolerant, pluralist, open to dissent, welcoming to artists and writers, committed to aesthetic experience rather than Babbitry, rooted in particular places but wide-ranging in affiliations and sympathies. Even Van Vechten, that arch-Menckenite who wrote in *The Tattooed Countess* of the "narrow prejudices" of the "cursed town" of his Iowa youth, called elsewhere for the artistic revision of his native land:

> There is, indeed, a feeling abroad that the Iowa scene is unworthy of description, as Iowa is usually imagined as a fecund but unbeautiful state laid out in flat squares. The contrary is the case. This fair land is unusually personal in its appeal and its beauty, which may not be immediately appreciated by those who glance at it casually from the back of an observation car on the Overland Limited, in the end proves to be haunting.[74]

American Gothic pointed to liberation from the terrible Puritanism that crushed enjoyment and beauty in so many American places.

This is the irony of the painting's initial fame: that its critique of Americans' widespread hostility to art was a source of its immediate popularity. Or, as the *Los Angeles Times*'s critic snappily put it, "presto—initiate and Philistine both like it." Looking at *American Gothic* in their newspapers, over breakfast or on the commuter train, in apartments, offices, automats, speakeasies, or on Main Streets (where real-life Carol Kennicotts couldn't imagine that Mencken was referring to them when he ridiculed boobs and ignoramuses), Americans who aspired, sometimes ambivalently, to be modern—to be emancipated and urbane—confirmed this image of themselves against the anachronisms gazing back at them.[75]

ICON

The 39 million visitors to A Century of Progress, the 1933–1934 World's Fair in Chicago, were treated to a celebration of modernity. Paul Philippe Cret's art deco Hall of Science, the fair's centerpiece, featured a 175-foot carillon tower that rang out with electrically played chimes. "Science Shoots Skyward," proclaimed a youth's guide to the fair beneath a photograph of the Sky-Ride that crossed the lagoon between the Hall of Science and Raymond Hood's Electrical Group, where a bas relief announced "The Conquest of Time and Space" and "Westinghouse" was emblazoned in red, white, blue, and amber lights on eight 70-foot towers. Just north, the General Motors building housed a full-scale Chevrolet assembly line. Not to be outdone, the 7-acre Chrysler complex included a test track, and Firestone exhibited a tire factory. "The foremost industries of the United States have mobilized their forces to tell the story of progress in transportation, communication and manufacturing of all kinds," declared a souvenir program, "and the beneficial results to humanity from their development."[76]

Although science and industry dominated the fair, the arts had a prominent place too. A photo of the Art Institute, the site of the fair's Exhibition of Paintings and Sculpture, appeared on the first page of the official program. If the organizers found it more difficult to dramatize the fair's theme of progress in a fine arts display—they weren't prepared to say, for example, that Miro's *Dog Barking at the Moon* represented an onward and upward movement from Titian's *Venus and the Lute Player*—they tried nonetheless. The point wasn't to trace aesthetic advancement but to celebrate "a hundred years' progress in American collecting."

In 1833 very few great works were on this side of the Atlantic; today the United States possesses treasures of amazing quality, inspiring not only to our artists but to the rapidly growing public who are coming to feel the need of art in their daily lives. Particularly during the last twenty-five or thirty years many brilliant examples of painting have made their way westward, some going at once into the museums, more finding their way into private hands. One of the chief aims of the present showing is to exhibit works which are rarely if ever seen by the public, emphasizing in this way the resources of the nation.

As science shot skyward, art collecting flowed westward, revealing the nation's cultural coming of age in terms of consumption if not production—"the complete progress of artistic appreciation in America" since the nineteenth century, in the words of one critic. Seven-hundred thousand visitors paid a quarter each to visit the second-floor galleries at the 1933 exhibition between June and November; another 800 thousand visited the free part of what the *Official World's Fair Weekly* called "the greatest art show—without a bit of rhetorical exaggeration—that America has ever seen."[77]

A second five-month show in 1934 took a more emphatic stance of cultural nationalism. "This year native achievement is the theme," the catalogue explained. Now "the characteristics and development of American painting from the eighteenth century to today" were on display.[78]

By almost all accounts, the most popular attraction at the 1933 exhibition was Whistler's "Mother"—*Arrangement in Gray and Black, No. 1*—the only painting on display not from an American collection. Loaned by the Louvre to the Museum of Modern Art in the fall of 1932, it had visited San Francisco, St. Louis, and Columbus, Ohio, before armed federal troops escorted it, "with all the pomp and ceremony befitting this treasured work of art," from Chicago's Union Station to the Art Institute on May 29, 1933. "The first query propounded when the visitor finds himself or herself inside the Art Institute," noted an observer, "is 'Where is Whistler's "Mother"?'"— except for the occasional confused visitors who asked where they could find the "whistling mother," "Whittier's Mother," or "Hitler's Mother." The millionth visitor to the exhibition received a framed print of the public's favorite. "You've seen it reproduced hundreds of times," enthused a newspaper guide to the show, "but had you ever hoped to enjoy this glorious masterpiece on your native soil?"[79]

One of two paintings on display valued at over a million dollars—the other was El Greco's *The Assumption of the Virgin*—*Arrangement in Gray and Black, No. 1* (1870–1871) was on the market for $1,200 in the United States in 1880 and sold in Paris in 1891 for less than $1,000. Seen by many viewers as a sentimental "Symbol of Motherhood" (or of "America's 'dear old mother complex,'" in the Menckenesque phrase of *Chicago Daily News* critic C. J. Bulliet), the painting became the exhibition's "shrine for the multitudes."[80]

The exhibition's second most popular American painting, according to Bulliet (*the* most popular, according to Thomas Craven, another critic who helped make Wood's national reputation), was *American Gothic*. For this, "with a blush of modest confusion," Bulliet took much of the credit. "I admit starting the furor," he wrote in the thirty-first of his daily columns (soon compiled as a guidebook titled *Art Masterpieces in a Century of Progress Fine Arts Exhibition at the Art Institute of Chicago*), "by 'discovering' the picture and rushing into print a reproduction all over the front page of the art magazine section of the old *Chicago Evening Post*. Requests for photographs of the painting began pouring in from newspapers and magazines all over the country, the high talent of the 'new master' being apparent even in newspaper reproduction." More prints of *American Gothic* were reportedly sold at A Century of Progress than of any other painting, including Whistler's "Mother."[81]

Since the initial ballyhoo in 1930 and 1931, *American Gothic* had been on display across the country. In San Diego, a critic heard "gurgles of appreciation" for "that pair of Puritan Iowa farmers" and praised "the authenticity of this social document" that had understandably—because it was so "convincing"—provoked resentment among the types it portrayed. "You can imagine a crowd of angry Iowans carrying Grant Wood's 'American Gothic' to a bonfire for the man has done something that touches the uninitiated." What many of the "uninitiated" saw and admired in the painting at the Chicago World's Fair may well have been different from what Bulliet and other critics had in mind. Reflecting on the fair, the *Des Moines Register* joined Craven in decreeing *American Gothic* "probably the most popular canvas on exhibit at A Century of Progress." Acknowledging that the painting "was not received without protest" in 1930, the *Register* observed that "in it many saw the flowering of real American art, sprung from American soil." Though it had often been "mistaken for an Iowa farmer and his wife, it really is a small town man and his daughter, some place in America." By 1933, the emphasis had begun to veer from the *Gothic* in the title to the *American*— from the iconoclastic to the iconic.[82]

It is hard to look back on A Century of Progress without a sense of irony. This unabashed paean to a streamlined, abundant America produced by visionary, public-spirited corporations took place at the height of the Great Depression. In 1933, with the gross national product half of what it had been before the Crash, steel and automobile production and farm income all down by close to two-thirds of 1929 levels, a quarter of the work force—thirteen million people—unemployed, progress was far from self-evident. The irony didn't escape some contemporaries. At the agricultural exhibits, *New Republic* critic Bruce Bliven observed crowds of "sunburned, silent, bashful men" who seemed numbly unaware of the incongruity of "arrays of huge, bright-painted new machines for increasing production, when already more is being produced than people can buy." With unconcealed Menckenesque disdain for "the great Middle Western middle class," benighted by their "dully passionate" version of "American Puritanism," Bliven perceived among the fairgoers no "mood of drastic impatience, of real desire to change things fundamentally," but only complacency or resignation:

> So far as I can see, the only future they envisage, as they plod wearily about the grounds and uncomplainingly pay nickel after nickel for entry to the lavatories, is one very like their past. More automobiles, with better gadgets; television added to their radios (television is demonstrated at the Fair). Maybe better banks, with less stock-market gambling and sharper control over "them big capitalists in Wall Street." And, undoubtedly, more Centuries of Progress to come to. . . .[83]

For the fair's organizers, as the historian Robert Rydell has argued, guarding against the drastic impatience that Bliven wished he had seen was precisely the point. "The century-of-progress fairs"—in Chicago, San Francisco, New York, and

elsewhere—"represented a powerful defense of corporate capitalism as a modernizing agency that would lead America out of
the depression towards a bountiful future"; they were
"designed to restore popular faith in the vitality of the nation's
economic and political system."[84]

Had Bliven visited the Art Exhibition, had he looked at
American Gothic in the company of people "who serve the
salad at the beginning of the meal and drink their coffee from
gigantic cups one-third full of cream" while remaining uncon-
scious "of the acute misery which their own social workers
report is going on among the poor in their own territory," he
might have seen in Wood's painting two exemplars of those
dully passionate Puritanical midwestern crowds. But what did
the crowds themselves see? In the absence of any recorded
impressions of visitors other than art critics, we can only speculate. Even Eleanor Roosevelt, whose surprise visit to the Art
Institute on October 31, 1933, gave the crowds "an unex-
pected thrill," didn't find time to comment after her "very hec-
tic but very interesting" trip to A Century of Progress.[85]

In the context of a fair that countered the dislocations of
the Depression with a vision of stability, order, and continuity—that provided "crisis-torn America with a cultural safety
net," in Rydell's phrase[86]—an earnest *American Gothic*
emerged to supplant its ironic predecessor. The old-fashioned
figures, those objects of ridicule among the knowing disciples
of Mencken, come to embody an enduring, essential American
spirit. No longer anachronistic, they are upright and steadfast,
determined to overcome hard times and fearlessly forge ahead
into the future. Depression-era viewers do not look down on
the man and woman; they look up to them, see their best
selves in them.

After the second world's fair exhibition closed, *American Gothic* traveled to the Ferargil Gallery for Wood's first one-man show in New York. Reviewed favorably in *Time* and *Newsweek*, the show also drew praise from the *New York American*, which described it as "a stirring spectacle" that reflected "the American spirit": "If you love America, you will love this show." The important critic Gilbert Seldes expressed his admiration too by shrewdly asking "whether the public response to his work does not reflect the social changes through which we are proceeding." For Seldes, Wood's paintings —*American Gothic* in particular—performed the important cultural work of transvaluing the pioneer past, ridiculed by the Menckenites, and recovering it for purposes of cultural continuity during the Depression. "Do we feel that Grant Wood is calling us back to a simplicity, and even a hardness, which has disappeared?" Seldes wondered. "It is notable that many of his paintings suggest the pioneer, as if they had been done before 1890; many of them are pictures of the middle-aged, of men and women stern and marked by suffering." In a "time of despair," Seldes wrote, "the pitchfork in the hand of his gaunt and decent 'Gothic' man may be taken as a weapon as well as a tool." He later remarked that Wood never meant the painting to be "a mean commentary on American life," even though it had been taken that way. A caption below a reproduction of *American Gothic* in the *Literary Digest* in August 1932 simply stated "Hearts of gold beat beneath the bleak exteriors in this canvas by Grant Wood," whereas the *Review of Reviews*' caption in January 1935 was more expansive: "PIONEER: American democracy was built upon the labors of men and women of stout hearts and firm jaws, such people as those above, painted by Grant Wood." *American*

Gothic would remind Americans that they possessed the heart, the stoutness and firmness, "the stern integrity combined with genuine productiveness," as *Scholastic* magazine characterized the image for the nation's high school students, to save American democracy.[87]

Hostile critics, especially critics from the left, saw the same populist nationalism, the same celebration of pioneer virtues—Seldes's weapons against the Depression—as a capitulation at best, an apology at worst. "With the capitalist class forced on the defensive by the ever-deepening crisis," Stephen Alexander observed in *New Masses*, "the need for bolstering its cracking economic foundations has been reflected in its frantic patrioteering in the cultural fields." Wood had ridden "the rising tide of national chauvinism to become the country's 'best seller,' and one of its most influential artists" by ignoring the ugly realities of the Depression in favor of a banal "Americanism."

One may perhaps wonder why Mr. Wood, who certainly knows about farming and the Middle West, having lived there most of his life, should paint only rich, prosperous farms, with spick-and-span new buildings, fat cattle, fine, fertile crops, and peaceful and contented farmers . . . when we've been reading so much these last several years about farm foreclosures, milk strikes, pitched battles between farmers and state troopers, sheriffs' sales, etc. You'd think that if he were so concerned about truth, authenticity, and honesty, he might have included some of these things in his pictures of Iowa farm country and people.

Spared the worst of the Depression, Iowa farmers nonetheless endured their share of the hardships that Alexander listed. The Iowa writer Curtis Harnack remembered the sight of striking farmers in 1932 and 1933 "waving pitchforks" at roadblocks they'd set up to enforce their "Farmer's Holiday" embargo and try to drive prices up. He also remembered the near lynching of Judge Charles Bradley, dragged from the LeMars courtroom where he issued foreclosure notices. "Prior to stringing him up on a light pole," Harnack wrote, "the farmers had stripped off his trousers and underwear and daubed his testicles with axle grease from a hubcap. Pulling out a knife, they threatened castration. They meant to scare him, not kill him, and Bradley did not die."[88]

When radical artists gathered in New York's Town Hall in February 1936 for the Communist Party–sponsored American Artists' Congress, they listened to Edward Rowan's successor as director of the Little Gallery in Cedar Rapids—the place that had nurtured the creation of *American Gothic* six years earlier—try to distance himself from Wood and his alleged flight from reality. "In presenting the case of Iowa," said Francis Robert White, "it is first necessary to discard the popularized version of the bucolic painter, milk pail in hand, and to realize that serious painters here as elsewhere are confronted with realities and are responsive to them." Not all Iowa artists felt "prompted to make pseudo-romantic halos out of the circumstances" of the Depression, and "they are not necessarily corn-conscious in their approach to art."[89]

Wood's paintings were popular, these critics observed, because they were reassuring. "Does he not corroborate the general wish-dream that after all everything is quite all right?" asked Lincoln Kirstein in *Art Front*. "His sweet, encompassable, diminutive landscapes, his quaint, sturdy, healthy folk, his well-kept, clean-smelling farm buildings give constant testimony that, in spite of all, we have our rocks and rills." Having made his own lasting contribution to American culture the year before by co-founding with George Balanchine what would become the New York City Ballet, Kirstein wasn't willing to give up on Wood. But his work would need to become much more challenging: genuinely *gothic* rather than vapidly American.

> He will have to cauterize that charm which, no matter how accurately he paints, clouds truth. And more than any mere technical mastery, he will have to gain some trace of insight into the real weather of his Middle West—dust storms and drought, slaughtered pigs, unsown crops or crops ploughed under. An element of tragedy would make his cleanly farmers less quaint, but closer to the spirit of the Gothic, which is no less beautiful because it is so grim.

The "grim-visaged" image of 1930 was apparently no longer grim enough for the times. It had evolved into "sentimental symbolism." Its keynote was "an optimism compounded of many moods and messages": "National birth and rebirth"; "Well-being"; "Survival." Celebrated for "producing an art that is real, indigenous to the life of his people" by his friend and fellow midwestern artist John Steuart Curry, Wood was simultaneously castigated by social realists for producing "an art that only deals with the good old days, walks backwards and brags of its unwillingness to expand" while consoling American society "with ideas of national superiority." Paraphrasing

FDR's inaugural address, a *New Republic* critic summed up the comforting message of Wood's work: "There is nothing to fear from an unfamiliar idiom in the painting, and hence nothing to fear from the unfamiliar conditions of the times."[90]

Wanda Corn has suggested that the perception of *American Gothic* as a satire "originated in the early 1930s on the East Coast and has been conventional historical wisdom ever since." But what about those Iowa farmwives, the painting's earliest critics, who certainly thought they were being satirized? And what about Seldes, Alexander, and Kirstein, East Coast critics who by the middle of the decade concluded that *American Gothic* was sentimental or celebratory rather than satirical? The most significant differences in understandings of *American Gothic* were not geographic but temporal. Its meanings shifted dramatically through the 1930s to the point where those who continued to see it as satirical were defying the conventional wisdom.[91]

Wood's public self-fashioning in these years contributed to the recasting of *American Gothic* into an image of reassuring nationalism. Like other artists and intellectuals during the Depression, he broadcast his redis-covery of America—though without the embrace of radical politics that characterized the "exiles' return" announced by the critic Malcolm Cowley. "I have found that a real world exists after all—," wrote the returning expatriate Harold Stearns, "and that world is my own country, from which I have been away far too long." Matthew Josephson put it more collectively and politically: "We turn back after the lapse of a whole misled generation; we return, literally, to face the American scene with our hopes and demands."[92]

Never really an expatriate, Wood described his return as a casting off of the foreign ways he had assumed on his trips to Europe—and as a rejection of bohemianism and Menckenism.

> I lived in Paris a couple of years myself and grew a very spectacular beard that didn't match my face or my hair, and read Mencken and was convinced that the Middle West was inhibited and barren. But I came back because I learned that French painting is very fine for French people and not necessarily for us, and because I started to analyze what it was I really knew. I found out. It's Iowa.

Renouncing the inauthenticity of "dreamy, old world landscapes after the manner of French Impressionists" and the affectations of what *Time* described as the "flaming pair of pink whiskers" and the "*beret basque*" of his Parisian days, Wood now fashioned himself as America's "artist in overalls"— dressed the same as the man in his signature painting—who had realized in his period of deracination that "all the good ideas I'd ever had came to me while I was milking a cow." Under Mencken's influence, wrote the critic Thomas Craven, Wood had "revolted against the Babbittry of his people, their arrogance and their indifference to the refinements of the spirit," had become alienated from his native soil—"persuaded to separate art and life"—but came back to become "the only American artist who is perfectly adjusted to his surroundings." (Mencken was puzzled by Wood's frequent references to him in speeches and interviews—to his recollections of the sway that the heartland bashing of "good old Mencken" had once held over him—and wrote to the artist seeking clarification. "In what way did I influence you precisely?" he asked, reassuring Wood that "this is not an objection but simply an inquiry." Mencken insisted that he shouldn't be held responsible for Wood's "emigration to Paris," since he had consistently denounced expatriation. "It seemed to me idiotic to go abroad, even for a painter," he explained, "and I certainly said so plainly enough.")[93]

In 1935, Wood painted a self-portrait that he called *Return from Bohemia*—intended for the cover of an autobiography of the same title—in which he looks up earnestly from his easel

In Return from Bohemia *(1935), Wood depicted himself as firmly re-rooted in the Midwest. [Curtis Galleries, Minneapolis, Minnesota]*

American Gothic, 1930, by Grant Wood. Oil on beaver board, 30 11/16 x 25 11/16 in. (78 x 65.3 cm) unframed. FRIENDS OF AMERICAN ART COLLECTION, 1930.934. REPRODUCTION, THE ART INSTITUTE OF CHICAGO.

Wood sketched the house on the spot in Eldon in August 1930. SMITHSONIAN AMERICAN ART MUSEUM, WASHINGTON, DC / ART RESOURCE, NY. © ESTATE OF GRANT WOOD / LICENSED BY VAGA, NEW YORK, NY.

The Beverly Hillbillies on the cover of *The Saturday Evening Post* in 1963. Irene Ryan, who played Granny, called her framed copy of the cover her "most treasured possession."

"Families that slay together stay together!" Blood drips from Yvonne DeCarlo's knife and Rod Steiger's pitchfork as terrified victims await their fate behind the window in this promotional image for the 1988 horror movie *American Gothic.*

An early presidential parody:
Lady Bird and Lyndon Johnson as
the *American Gothic* couple on a
comedy record. REPRISE RECORDS

Hillary and Bill Clinton by Alfred
Gescheidt, master of the presidential
parody. PHOTOGRAPH © ALFRED GESCHEIDT

That isn't corn they're growing behind the *American Gothic* house on the cover of the "Grass Roots" installment of *The Fabulous Furry Freak Brothers* in 1977. COVER ART FOR *THE FABULOUS FURRY FREAK BROTHERS IN "GRASS ROOTS"* BY GILBERT SHELTON AND DAVE SHERIDAN. COPYRIGHT © 1977, 2004 BY GILBERT SHELTON. ORIGINAL, ENGLISH LANGUAGE PUBLICATION 1977 BY RIP OFF PRESS, INC. IN SAN FRANCISCO, CALIFORNIA, USA. BY PERMISSION FROM GILBERT SHELTON.

Baby Boomers as the new quintessential Americans on the cover of an accounting firm's promotional materials in 2003. BRIAN J. WILLSE

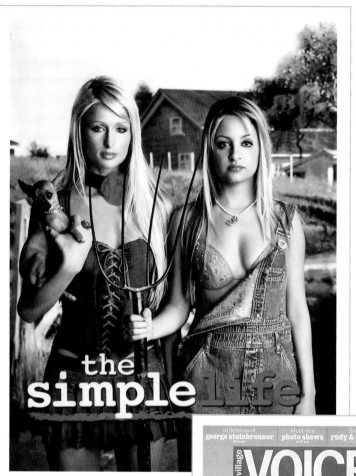

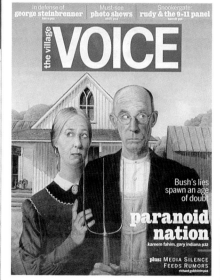

Paris Hilton and Nicole Richie
scandalize middle America in their
"reality" show *The Simple Life*.
THE SIMPLE LIFE PHOTO PROVIDED COURTESY
OF FOX BROADCASTING COMPANY.

American Gothic again stands for the
nation, now "paranoid" as the Bush
administration fights the war on terror.
COPYRIGHT © 2004 VILLAGE VOICE MEDIA, INC.
REPRINTED WITH THE PERMISSION OF *THE
VILLAGE VOICE*.

A European views the United States through *American Gothic*. George W. Bush skewers Iraq and Afghanistan with Tony Blair standing by his side and Osama bin Laden looming in the background in an anti-war collage by an English-born resident of Turkey. MICHAEL DICKINSON, *AMERICAN GOTHIC 2*, HTTP://CARNIVAL_OF_CHAOS.TRIPOD.COM

and palette, his brow furrowed, a deep cleft in his clean-shaven chin ("a sturdy, foursquare son of the Middle West," Craven called him), surrounded by Iowans, young and old, who bow their heads reverently behind the people's artist and his canvas, with a barn standing tall in the background. Having "built for himself a bridge back to America," in Gilbert Seldes's admiring account, Wood was "digging himself in," rooting his work in "the center of America" and "getting arresting beauty out of common things, to which we have long been indifferent." In the midst of massive economic and social dislocation, Wood and his paintings came across as settled, at home, authentic. "Authenticity is his fetish," *Newsweek* pronounced:

> He consults mail order catalogues on the exact design of farm implements, carefully checks the detailed differences among breeds of domestic animals, and even the kind of hay in his painted wagons. When at last he goes to work, Wood drives himself for seven or eight weeks, painting as long as fourteen hours a day.

Here was the artist as craftsman, unalienated from his materials and his labor, who had once "raised a French beard" but, starting with *American Gothic*, now raised paintings as farmers raised corn, producing culture out of the soil, like agriculture, "a perfectly natural phenomenon," as Seldes described him, a believer in "the application of hard labor to all art," according to a 1935 exhibition catalog, with a "wholesome, usually optimistic" outlook. (Wood's devotees in the 1930s would have been puzzled by the description of "American Gothic" blend coffee at the Java House in Iowa City, which I have sampled and found delicious. "Robust earthiness" seems right, but "a

Grant Wood as a bohemian in Paris with "flaming pink whiskers." [Collection of Figge Art Museum]

classic French roast"?) Wood and his art were, in the stabiliz-ing terms of Depression-era cultural nationalism, real, sin-cere, indigenous, native.[94]

They were also masculine. A historian of facial hair observed in 1930 that "the simple possession of a beard is enough to mark as curious any young man who has the courage to grow one." Wood's shaving of his "flaming" whiskers and casting off of his beret—and, more importantly, his well-publicized declarations of independence from effete European and eastern influences, his turn from the artificial-ity of impressionist imitations in Paris to what *Time* called "his natural style, hard, exact, brittle"—linked authenticity to gender. For all the "feminine" qualities of Wood's spherical trees and rolling hills, his admirers, like Seldes, tended to emphasize the "hardness" of his work, and in the mythic biography Wood constructed for himself, he accentuated his move from "artificial precepts" to "more vital human experience,"

The artist as sturdy citizen. [Peter A. Juley & Son Collection, Smithsonian American Art Museum, J0002303]

from the "soft and mellow" to the "hard" and "solid." This rhetoric was, of course, much more restrained than the rants of his friend Thomas Hart Benton (who returned from New York to his native Missouri in 1935 on Wood's advice) against the "control" of the art world by "precious fairies" with "predilections for the curving wrist and outthrust hip." Benton urged artists to escape the East—to repudiate "those aesthetic orthodoxies, cults, and conformist principles which in the great cities tend to sterilize expression"—and to fortify themselves by immersion in "the realities of common life." When Wood remarked that he had tried to make the people in *American Gothic* "more like themselves than they were in actual life," he was asserting that his likenesses were even more real than reality.[95]

The figure of the unbent, determined, evidently *working* man (working, if not with his pitchfork, then in town, judging from the prosperous appearance of his clothes, house, and barn) had particular resonance amid the Depression's upheaval in gender relations. In the Levi Strauss warehouse in San Francisco, a six-month supply of 501 Double X denim overalls, 120,000 pairs, lay unsold in 1931 as Levi's primary customers for their staple product—farmers, factory workers, and miners—lost their incomes. With massive unemployment, the traditional male role as breadwinner was under siege. "Before the depression, I wore the pants in the family, and rightly so," confessed an unemployed man in 1940. "During the depression, I lost something. Maybe you call it self-respect, but in losing it I also lost the respect of my children, and I am afraid that I am losing my wife." Marriage and birth rates fell dramatically. One response to the crisis was to enshrine those traditional roles in public visual culture.

Whether the man in *American Gothic* is the woman's father or husband, the two figures' roles are both complementary and clearly differentiated. He carries the tool and wears the overalls; she wears an apron. He performs the paid labor; she keeps house. They stand next to each other, and maybe they display the "sense of satisfying mutual endeavor" that characterized what historian Barbara Melosh calls "the comradely ideal" of much Depression-era public art. But the woman also stands behind the man. He looks resolutely straight ahead; she looks away, her fortitude dependent on his. Patriarchy remains visibly intact in the painting.[96]

Wood's discovery of his native soil, the critic Arthur Millier perceptively noted in 1940, "was a story that went beyond the bounds of a merely personal experience and became a significant chapter in the history of American culture. For what happened to Grant Wood has been happening to a whole generation of American artists and writers and musicians."[97] The Depression-era search for rootedness—"for some transcendent identification with a mythic America" in the historian Warren Susman's formulation—manifested itself in a variety of endeavors to connect with "the people." As the figures in *American Gothic* transmuted from nasty Puritans to hardy folk, they joined in diverse efforts to document the lives of "ordinary" Americans and discover or preserve a usable national past. Woody Guthrie's *Dust Bowl Ballads*, John Steinbeck's *The Grapes of Wrath* (and John Ford's film adaptation), Erskine Caldwell and Margaret Bourke-White's *You Have Seen Their Faces*, Paul Taylor and Dorothea Lange's *An American Exodus*, James Agee and Walker Evans's *Let Us Now Praise Famous Men* recorded the struggles of southern sharecroppers and tenant farmers. Richard Wright in *Twelve Million Black Voices*, Edmund Wilson in *American Jitters*, James Rorty in *Where Life is Better*, Theodore Dreiser in *Tragic America*, Sherwood Anderson in *Puzzled America*, and other writers and intellectuals took to the road to "experience" the social and economic conditions of the Depression. Some of these efforts blurred the lines between the Communist-inflected radicalism of the Popular Front and the officially sanctioned populism of the federal arts projects. Alan Lomax's exhaustive recordings for the Library of Congress Archive of American Folk Song (which included the work of Guthrie and Leadbelly, both of whom were involved with left-wing politics) captured an extraordinary range of what we now call "roots" music. The Federal Writers' Project produced a massive archive of oral histories—invaluable narratives of former slaves among them—and the American Guide Series, in which more than 6,000 researchers and writers described the culture, history, and geography of each of the forty-eight states. Lange and Evans, along with Arthur Rothstein, Carl Mydans, Russell Lee, John Vachon, Jack Delano, Marion Post Wolcott, Gordon Parks, and other photographers working for Roy Stryker in the Farm Security Administration's Historical Division, created the images in which we still see the Depression. The Federal Art Project assembled an archive of American folk art, the *Index of American Design*. Painters employed by the Public Works of Art Project (PWAP) and the Treasury Section of Painting and Sculpture (later the Section of Fine Arts) decorated post offices and other public buildings with murals that often depicted idyllic scenes from the American past.[98]

The left's critical populism emphasized conflict—especially the conflict between labor and capital, but also racial and ethnic pluralism. As the historian Michael Denning has observed, "the 'people' invoked by the left-wing Popular Front were neither the vast 'middle' between the economic royalists and the foreign 'lower classes' nor the white, ethnically unmarked, forgotten men: they were working men and women of many races and nationalities." The affirmative, consensual populism of the New Deal's official culture downplayed difference and division in conjuring a harmonious American people and providing, in Susman's phrase, "a sense of belonging and belief in an era of shame and fear." When Edward Bruce, director of the Section of Fine Arts, introduced an exhibit of New Deal mural designs and sculptures at Washington's Corcoran Gallery in November 1939, he voiced the role of art in fostering a spirit of patriotic affirmation. "The national art of a country reflects with unerring accuracy the character of its people," Bruce declared, "and the character that looks out from these walls gives one a very contented feeling about this dear country of ours." The exhibit offered "a panorama of America triumphant, clear-eyed and unafraid." Wood, the painter of those clear-eyed and unafraid middle Americans standing in front of their well-kept house with its aspiring gothic window, flanked by smoothly rounded trees and their neat red barn, under cloudless blue skies, increasingly spoke the same language of stouthearted Americanism. He served as Iowa state director of the PWAP in 1934 and supervised the painting of a series of "Practical Arts" murals under PWAP auspices at Iowa State University. His friend Edward Rowan moved from Cedar Rapids to Washington to work as an administrator under Edward Bruce at the Section of Fine Arts, where he played an important role in vetting the designs for post office murals.[99]

If Wood's images of wholesome midwestern rural life helped shape the aesthetic standards of the federal arts projects, those projects in turn helped transform *American Gothic*. It speaks to the power of the cultural New Deal that those gaunt figures could be absorbed into the iconography of the post office murals and other public works of art. I would go so far as to say that the figures' bodies and faces changed as they took their places within the New Deal's ubiquitous imagery of "frontier hardiness and pastoral virtue"—not so much as to turn into the muscled men and buxom women of some rural-themed murals, but enough to become one of the "stalwart" farm couples who populated almost all of them and served as what Melosh calls "visual icons of heroic common people, mutuality, and purposeful labor."[100]

This reimagination of *American Gothic* also has to be considered in light of Wood's subsequent work, especially his landscapes. *Stone City, Iowa* (1930)—a painting of the tiny Wapsipinicon River valley town where Wood would establish a short-lived artists' colony and school in 1932—followed by *Young Corn* (1931), *Fall Plowing* (1931), *Arbor Day* (1932), and *Spring Turning* (1936), depicted an idyll of order, self-sufficiency, and agricultural abundance. *Fruits of Iowa* (1932), his panels for the coffee shop at the Montrose Hotel in Cedar Rapids, featured extraordinarily robust farmers, cows, chickens, pigs, geese, corn, melons, beans, cabbages, and other fruits and vegetables. James Dennis locates these paintings, with their independent yeomen, their carefully plotted and meticulously maintained fields, fences, roads, and lines of trees, their bounteous produce, within a resonant tradition of Jeffersonian agrarianism—an "ideology based on an Edenic ideal" that "invariably reappeared during periods of discontent." Wood's farms and farmers appear blissfully unconnected to the market economy, but it would be a stretch to see in them a critique of industrial capitalism. Freedom from fear through a national pastoral myth is their dominant note.[101]

Wood died of pancreatic cancer in February 1942. Seeking a fittingly gothic ending to his life, critic Richard Davenport-Hines claims that Wood was a "living exemplification of the double man." In demand as a lecturer across the country, unable to reconcile his role as a nationally renowned leader of the "American Scene" movement in art with his commitment to his own work and his own region, Wood was torn apart, Davenport-Hines surmises, driven to despair and an early death. "The couple in *American Gothic* have become as instantly recognisable figures as *Mona Lisa*, or van Gogh's self-portrait, or Warhol's *Marilyn*," writes Davenport-Hines in *Gothic: Four Hundred Years of Excess, Horror, Evil and Ruin*; "the swift and phenomenal fame of this painting trapped Wood in an unresolvable dilemma." If one is going to speculate about Wood's torments in the late 1930s and early 1940s, however, the politics of his teaching job, his financial troubles, the unraveling of his marriage, and his unresolved sexuality are more plausible candidates than an internalized conflict between region and nation. He was certainly unhappy in the spring and early summer of 1941, when he was fighting with colleagues in the art department at the University of Iowa, whom he charged with "defamation," "maladministration, bohemianism and intrigue." But after the department was reorganized to his satisfaction, he enjoyed "a magnificent summer," "the best in many, many years." At his retreat in Clear Lake, he savored "peace of mind."[102]

Wood's self-styled regionalism—he was increasingly identified in these years with Benton of Missouri and Curry of Kansas as one of painting's "Regionalist Triumvirate"—was largely indistinguishable from the therapeutic cultural nationalism of the New Deal. Neither the regionalist painters nor the participants in the New Deal's arts projects viewed the rediscovery of local or regional cultures as an end in itself. Both sought the nation through the region, just as the first self-conscious collectors of American folk art, seeking the New England roots of American civilization, had done at the beginning of the colonial revival movement in the 1880s. Until the New Deal, efforts to collect and catalog early American furniture, textiles, paintings, carvings, metalwork, ceramics, baskets, tools, and toys had been private and piecemeal. In 1935, the Federal Arts Project launched the *Index of American Design*, an ambitious attempt to document American folk art in all its local and regional forms. The *Index*'s organizers likewise saw unity rather than diversity as the project's justification and goal. Holger Cahill, the FAP director, spoke of folk art as "varied" but above all as "an honest and straightforward expression of the spirit of a people"—"an authentic expression of American experience." Constance Rourke, the folklorist who served as the *Index*'s editor—and a much more subtle regionalist thinker than Wood—posited something or someone she called "the American type," an underlying "structural truth" or "singular unity," the essence of which or whom transcended "its many variations." Wood's regionalist rhetoric sounded very much like Franklin Roosevelt's celebration of art that was no longer "something foreign" to Americans but "painted by their own kind in their own country, and painted about things they know and look at often and have touched and loved." Art, from this nationalist perspective, could embody, express, produce, and reproduce the nation. Though Wood insisted that "each section has a personality of its own" and that artists would "work out and interpret in their productions these varying personalities," he articulated a regionalism that elided the local and the national, the midwestern and the American.[103]

In his 1935 regionalist manifesto *Revolt Against the City*, Wood continued to distance himself from the 1920s' "revolt against the village" that had informed the painting and initial reception of *American Gothic*. The Depression, he wrote, had had the salutary effect of challenging Mencken and Sinclair Lewis's "contempt" for "the hinterland"—their "urban and European philosophy"—and replacing it with a healthier "American way of looking at things":

> The Great Depression has taught us many things, and not the least of them is self-reliance. It has thrown down the Tower of Babel erected in the years of a false prosperity; it has sent men and women back to the land; it has caused us to rediscover some of the old frontier virtues. In cutting us off from traditional but more artificial values, it has thrown us back upon cer-

tain true and fundamental things which are distinctively ours to use and exploit.

Wood satirized chauvinism in *Daughters of Revolution,* a painting of three primly self-assured D.A.R. women standing in front of Emmanuel Leutze's *Washington Crossing the Delaware* that stirred up some controversy in 1932. (Nan recalled that "Grant was sick and tired of a little clique of women who had done nothing in this world on their own, put on airs and considered themselves aristocrats and above us common folk, solely because they or their mother belonged to the D.A.R." Grant told a reporter that he had avoided the full wrath of professional patriots only by touting his American Legion membership and his own descent from colonial Americans, and he told Craven that he had a "low opinion" of *Daughters of Revolution,* presumably because it was the only time that he had "given vent to satire.") Yet despite his insistence that his patriotism was nothing more than "a feeling for one's own milieu and for the validity of one's own life and its surroundings" and that all regions had equal contributions to make in the "competition" that would produce "a rich American culture," Wood equated "true and fundamental"—the genuinely American—with the rural and small-town heartland. The East, the city, with their "confusing cosmopolitanism" were, by this calculus, incapable of furnishing the "native material" for an authentic national art.[104]

There is no way to date precisely when the Midwest came to represent "America," but the rhetoric and iconography of the Depression—and *American Gothic* in particular—certainly helped consolidate the association. As a term for the region comprising the twelves states of Kansas, Nebraska, Missouri,

Iowa, North and South Dakota, Minnesota, Wisconsin, Illinois, Indiana, Michigan, and Ohio, "Middle West" entered into popular usage around 1910. According to a geographer who studied articles about the region in popular magazines, the initial "reign of the Middle West as the self-confident symbol of the United States" extended through the 1910s, weathered the criticisms of the 1920s (when, for the debunkers, its undisputed "reign" over the nation was precisely why it needed debunking), and gained renewed force in the 1930s. Iowa, at the geographical middle of the Middle West, emerged as the heart of the heartland, the "epitome" of the region and, hence, the nation. Wood attributed a "wistful nostalgia for the Midwest" to "the alarming nature of the depression":

> This region has always stood as the great conservative section of the country. Now, during boom times conservatism is a thing to be ridiculed, but under unsettled conditions it becomes a virtue. To the East, which is not in a position to produce its own food, the Middle West today looks a haven of security.[105]

Inverting the conventional wisdom according to which the 1930s broke with the conservatism of the 1920s, Wood perceived that the predominant cultural response to the Depression—the powerful yearning for security—was more conservative than the debunking ethos of the boom.

Some 1930s' regionalists envisioned a radical restructuring of the American economy and political system, massive decentralization and resettlement, and a complete social and cultural reorientation. The critic and planner Lewis Mumford was one of them, and he recognized that Wood wasn't.

Reviewing Wood's Ferargil Gallery show in *The New Yorker*, Mumford asserted that this "great exponent of an indigenous art, the breaker of our slavish ties to Europe, the discoverer of native materials and native methods, the layer of new regional foundations for American painting," remained "a colonial of colonials" who hadn't yet created a painting— including *American Gothic*, "his best painting to date"—that wasn't "completely derivative in both symbol and technique from the Europe that the Middle West has supposedly thrown off." Like his friend Constance Rourke, Mumford didn't object to the premise of discovering or creating "a native art," but they shared the view that Wood "used superficial and transient elements of the American subject"—note the singular—"without touching its core." Having praised Benton only a few years earlier as "a fine talent, indigenous, humorous, satirical, moved by the actual tempo of modern life and savagely aware of its representative faces and attitudes," Mumford now saw in Benton's midwestern regionalist ally a reactionary aesthetics and politics that veered dangerously close to fascism. However unfair his judgment of Wood's work, Mumford astutely observed that in standing "for the corn-fed Middle West against the anemic East" Wood had "become a National Symbol for the patrioteers." His regionalism, Mumford charged, posed no genuine alternative to nationalism, provincialism, and corporate capitalism.[106]

Amid the initial controversy over *American Gothic*, Wood had pointed to the painting's title to argue that his figures were "American" rather than Iowan. By the mid-1930s, those Iowans had indeed become representative Americans. Wood and his fellow regionalists, the art historian Karal Ann Marling contends, were fully aware that in their deployment of the "native" and "authentic" they were seeking the "typical" rather than the "singular and unique." As "an art of national stereotypes," writes Marling, regionalism "constituted a powerful social bond between the painter and the people whose familiar, even conventional images of their America found confirmation and new resonance in his prim faces, his yards of rickrack, his red-flannel skivvies."[107] Painted before Wood adopted the regionalist label, *American Gothic* had initially resisted the identification of viewers with its subjects, and the bond between the painter and his public was constituted by their ironic distance from those prim faces.

When irony gave way to identification, when the figures in *American Gothic* became positive national stereotypes, the celebration of the "native" slipped into nativism. At the 1939 New York World's Fair, the "Typical American Families" display featured the winners of a national competition—winners came from all forty-eight states—in which local judges made their decisions based on contestants' essays and a questionnaire that asked, among other things, about each family's "racial origin." The winners were all native-born whites. "Nothing is more characteristic of the 1930s vision of the people," Warren Susman pointed out, "than the concept of the typical or the average," and the typical or the average was always white. The satirical *American Gothic* had depicted types without insisting that their typicality embodied an entire people; the ironic distance implied between viewer and subject meant that the figures could be descriptively but not normatively American. In other words, despite Wood's deprecation of "foreign influences," there is nothing inherently nativist about the image. It became nativist only when the couple came to stand for a resolute American nation. Like other efforts to embody the people, it offered the reassurance of unity, the collective sense of belonging that mitigated the dislocations of the Depression. Like these other efforts, it did so by representing America as white.[108]

In 1942, in Washington, D.C., Gordon Parks took his first professional photograph. In front of an enormous American flag hanging on the wall at the Farm Security Administration, Parks posed a black cleaning woman named Ella Watson. She looks directly at the camera through her wire-rimmed glasses, her expression serious but not grim. She wears a polka-dot dress that is neat but tattered, a small hole revealing the elastic at the waist. A mop stands to her left, probably balanced in a bucket on the floor. In her right hand, though the hand is outside the frame, she holds a broom, its bristles pointing upward to mirror the stripes of the flag. The title of the picture in the Library of Congress collection of FSA photographs is *Washington, D.C. Government Charwoman*, with the alternate title *Ella Watson*. Parks called it *American Gothic*.

He had bought his first camera in 1938 after seeing some FSA photos in a magazine someone had left on the *North Coast Limited*, a train that ran between Chicago and Seattle where he worked as a waiter. "These stark, tragic images of human beings caught up in the confusion of poverty saddened me," Parks recalled. "I took the magazine home and studied it for weeks." He also read Steinbeck's *In Dubious Battle*, Caldwell and Bourke-White's *You Have Seen Their Faces*, and "what became my Bible, *12 Million Black Voices*—a powerful statement against bigotry, with text by Richard Wright and photographs from the FSA files." On layovers in Chicago, he visited the Art Institute, "spending hours in this large voiceless place, studying paintings of Monet, Renoir and Manet." He must have seen Grant Wood's painting too. In 1940, determined to be a photographer, he moved to Chicago. "During that first year there my family learned to spell *suffer*. But just when food and money hit the zero mark, fate resurrected my hopes." The Julius Rosenwald Fund awarded him a fellowship on the basis of his photographs of Chicago's South Side, "where poverty ensnared the huge black population." The Rosenwald Fund brought his work to the attention of Roy Stryker, head of FSA's Photography Division, who invited him to Washington. "Sensing my ignorance," Parks recalled, Striker sent him out, without his camera, "to get acquainted with the rituals of the nation's capital."

Expecting the "radiant, historic" city "to be the one place where I could find democracy," Parks found instead that "racism was rampant." He was "shooed" to the back doors of restaurants, shut out of theaters, refused service at department stores. He hurried back to Stryker's office "like an angry wind."

I was furious. I wanted to photograph discrimination. Roy said, "You just don't go out and photograph discrimination. How do you do it? This is what you have to learn. I want you to sit down and write me a long set of plans about how you would attempt to do it." Of course, it was very difficult for me. I didn't know how to do it. Finally, he sent me to talk with a black charwoman who worked in the building. [In other accounts, Parks met her without Stryker's urging, when she was mopping the floor late that evening after everyone else had left the office.] "You will find out a lot from the lady," he said. And I did. I found out that she had

Gordon Parks's American Gothic, Ella Watson in Washington, D.C., 1942. *[Library of Congress, Prints & Photographs Division, FSA-OWI Collection, reproduction number LC-USF34-T01-013407-C DLC.]*

been a charwoman there for many years. Yet, she had been to high school, and she deserved a much better job. I took her into a room where there was an American flag draped on the wall. I posed her against it— Grant Wood style—with a mop in one hand and a broom in the other. When Roy saw that photograph, he said, "You're going to get us all fired."

Parks learned that "What the camera had to do was expose the evils of racism, the evils of poverty, the discrimination and the bigotry, by showing the people who suffered most under it." Washington, Parks decided, "could now have a conversation" with his portrait of Ella Watson. In posing a black charwoman in front of the central symbol of American nationalism—her stance, her expression, her broom, and his preferred title sharply punning on another, much newer symbol of this nationalism—Parks "had found a little justice." The normative whiteness of the now iconic *American Gothic* did not go unrecognized and unchallenged.[109]

Gordon Parks composed his *American Gothic* a month after Pearl Harbor, five months after Franklin Roosevelt issued Executive Order 8802, which outlawed employment discrimination in the defense industries, in response to A. Philip Randolph's promise of a mass protest march on Washington. In August 1941, anticipating U.S. entry into World War II, *Fortune* magazine proposed a series of war posters. Rejecting the crude Hun-hating images of World War I

—such images "would today do little more than arouse a strong nostalgia for the days when war was simple and unsubtle"—*Fortune* called for more sophisticated instruments of "propaganda and morale." Though posters remained a "cheap, efficient, and pliant" medium, propagandists had to be aware of the risks of "underestimating rather than overestimating the public taste." In *Fortune*'s view, "The American" (singular, male) "has matured in the quarter century that has carried him from one war to another. His knowledge is greater, his background broader, his taste stricter."

With these caveats in mind, *Fortune* offered as its first candidate for a World War II poster Grant Wood's *American Gothic*, framed against a black background and boldly captioned in white with the wartime words of Abraham Lincoln: "GOVERNMENT OF THE PEOPLE BY THE PEOPLE AND FOR THE PEOPLE SHALL NOT PERISH FROM THE EARTH." Belying its own notion of a monolithic "American," the magazine suggested careful marketing—an awareness that "posters can be designed for specific audiences."

> The poster on this page is an extreme example. Grant Wood's *American Gothic* becomes a folk piece, a symbol of the independent, don't tread on me character that Americans recognize as peculiarly American. *American Gothic* would be an unhappy choice for the walls of a munitions plant but for schools, banks, offices it might properly achieve a prominence that no orthodox poster could hope to equal.

If defense workers needed something less domestic, more martial, most others—of no very specific demographic profile

GOVERNMENT OF THE PEOPLE
BY THE PEOPLE AND FOR THE PEOPLE
SHALL NOT PERISH FROM THE EARTH

The American Gothic *figures have become determined
defenders of American democracy in* Fortune's *proposed
war poster, 1941. [*Fortune*]*

after all—would rally around the timely timelessness of this
icon of American toughness and exceptionalism. The painting
was perfect poster material, said the *Cedar Rapids Gazette* in a
piece subtitled "Grant Wood's 'American Gothic' Is Finally
Understood," because "good art would boost national morale
more than mediocre art." In the spring of 1941, Wood himself
insisted that art had an important role to play in national

defense: not "flag-waving" art with "screaming eagles and goddesses of liberty upholding flaming torches"; not "smart, sophisticated stuff" either; just paintings of "the simple, everyday things that make life significant to the average person." Pressed into national service during the Depression, the affirming, unironic *American Gothic* was prepared to join the fight in World War II.[110]

The Roosevelt administration ignored *Fortune*'s advice, and the painting never did become an official war poster. But *American Gothic* resonated during the war nonetheless. In May 1943, the *Chicago Tribune* reproduced *American Gothic* as an inspiration for the home front. "Beneath the stern and unyielding righteousness of men and women who conquered the soil of America," the *Tribune* intoned in its caption, "Grant Wood has depicted their fixed belief in a better tomorrow . . . an undying patriotism . . . a readiness to sacrifice, that their sons and daughters might go forward!"[111]

In 1944, Albert O. Olson of Glencoe, Illinois, printed a pamphlet titled *Stopping at Grant Wood's "American Gothic"* as a Christmas greeting from him and his wife, Laura. Olson explained to his friends that *American Gothic* was more than "a picture of a peaceful country setting." It conveyed "the national character" and possessed "universal significance. It speaks a message to the nation. It is the basis of American democracy, and is set in midwest America, the backbone of American strength." More than a picture, more than a representation, more even than a clear and direct speaker of truths, it *is*—as Olson's verbs slip from action to embodiment—the essence of the nation.

Olson had bought a full-size print for his home just after Wood's death in February 1942 and saw in the image the certainty that things would return to normal after the war. "The Germans may today slay a thousand Danes or two thousand Norwegians, but the man with the pitchfork knows that clover will blossom again and that he will have hay to pitch when the cows come home." The man with the pitchfork, which can serve "both as weapon and as a tool," represents the American will to fight for national and material security and progress. The nation, Olson wrote, "must rely on the men who will line up with 'The Man with the Fork.'"

> In all elemental essentials he is a successful man. He has a balanced mentality and is competent to receive a new idea with ease. He is not rich—but he is wealthy, without evidence of any bank account. His assets are one hundred percent—his liabilities none. His credit is unlimited with friend or stranger.

He embodies American individualism, the "Spirit of Enterprise," and the capitalist-Christian commitment to "service."

> He may now be hearing those resounding words spoken by the carpenter's Son, *"He who will save his life shall lose it."* And he may quietly answer without argument, but with full assurance from his work, *"But he who will use his life will find it."*

Having come to represent the pioneer spirit, patriotism, and faith in progress during the hard times of the 1930s, *American Gothic* again provided the stability of the timeless—the "fixed" and "undying"—amid the anxiety and flux of wartime.[112]

PARODY

There is an *American Gothic* moment in the 1957 Broadway hit *The Music Man*. Early in the second scene, as the audience is introduced to the show's setting of River City, Iowa, the townspeople sing of themselves,

> We can be cold as our falling thermometers in
>   December
> If you ask about our weather in July
> And we're so by God stubborn we can stand
>   touchin' noses
> For a week at a time and never see eye-to-eye
> But we'll give you our shirt

And a back to go with it
If your crops should happen to die.

Two workmen then leave a large packing case at center stage to frame a "farmer & wife" (according to the stage directions) who have entered from the wings and pose in a tableau of *American Gothic*. The farmer breaks the pose to sing "So what the heck, you're welcome/Glad to have you with us," and, together with his wife, "Even though we may not ever mention it again." [113]

The Music Man, like some other versions of *American Gothic*, is ambivalent about the Iowans it portrays. Harold Hill, the "slicker" traveling salesman and con artist who comes to River City to sell musical instruments and band uniforms even though he knows nothing about music, ends up winning the heart of Marian the librarian and transforming the town. His scam has brought "lights" and "flags" and "colors" and, of course, music—brought joy, in short, to leaven the town's "Iowa kind of special chip-on-the-shoulder attitude." He has saved the cultured Marian, who reads Chaucer, Rabelais, and Balzac—"advocates *dirty books*," say the town's puritanical women—from becoming an old maid. [114]

But if *American Gothic*'s appearance suggests the town's stubbornness and defensiveness, it also stands for River City's—and the show's—wholesome Americanism. After all, the townspeople are welcoming even though they're reserved and undemonstrative. Harold and Marian seem likely to stay, now that he has given up his wandering and dishonest ways. The show was "simple-minded and unsophisticated" but "also warmhearted, brilliantly performed and a lot of fun," *Time* magazine declared in a cover story that featured, as did *Life*'s

"So what the heck, you're welcome/Glad to have you with us/Even though we may not ever mention it again" sings the couple in the 1957 Broadway hit The Music Man. *[Life]*

photo spread, the "famous Iowa pose." *Time* quoted Brooks Atkinson's *New York Times* review, which glowingly tagged *The Music Man* "as American as apple pie and a Fourth of

July oration." (The beginning of the show, including the *American Gothic* tableau, takes place on July 4.) Meredith Willson, the author and composer, recounted his own childhood in "innocent Iowa," and Morton DaCosta, the director, pronounced that "the job of the theater is not to feed pessimism but to dispel it." The show's effect, *Time* determined, was "a sunny day-at-the-farm euphoria. In a fat Broadway season whose successes deal so clinically with such subjects as marital frustration, alcoholism, dope addiction, juvenile delinquency and abortion, *The Music Man* is a monument to golden unpretentiousness and wholesome fun."[115]

The show is set in 1912. That *American Gothic* wasn't painted for another eighteen years doesn't prevent the characters from assuming the pose. By 1957, after all, the image had ascended to timelessness—a symbol of enduring American wholesomeness echoed in the 1962 movie version and in countless revivals ever since.

Time, *Life*, and *The Music Man* were prime examples of what postwar intellectuals characterized, with a growing sense of alarm, as "mass culture": "homogenized," "mechanical," commodified, formulaic, depersonalized, "nerveless," "safe," "indifferent to standards"; "predigested" to elicit "vicarious experience and faked sensations," "Built-In Reactions" instead of demanding serious effort to produce individual responses; "cultural pap or gruel," "garbage," or "kitsch," the word that the art critic Clement Greenberg introduced to the American vocabulary in 1939. The dangers of mass culture, these intellectuals argued, were both aesthetic and political. Mass culture, not just bad art but "sub-art," "non-art," or even "anti-art," according to Dwight Macdonald, threatened by a kind of Gresham's Law to drive out high culture entirely, leaving in its place "a debased, permanent" pseudoculture devoid of significant "feelings, ideas, tastes, visions." Mass culture pointed toward totalitarianism by contributing to the creation of a "mass man," solitary without being individuated, "uniform with the millions of other atoms that go to make up 'the lonely crowd'" (David Riesman's best-seller of that title was published in 1950), a "non-man, that is man in a special relationship to other men that makes it impossible for him to function as man (one of the human functions being the creation and enjoyment of works of art)." "Mass Culture is not and can never be any good," Macdonald bluntly pronounced. "I take it as axiomatic that culture can only be produced by and for human beings. But in so far as people are organized (more strictly, disorganized) as masses, they lose their human identity and quality." The effect of mass culture was to "cretinize" or "brutalize" its consumers.[116]

American Gothic, its postwar detractors charged, belonged to mass culture's illegitimate offspring, middlebrow culture or "midcult." Like all kitsch, middlebrow culture was banal, but it had pretensions to significance and was often "able to pass itself off as the real thing." Greenberg placed Wood "among the notable vulgarizers of our period" and blamed him for peddling "an inferior product under the guise of high art." Though he didn't name *American Gothic* specifically, Macdonald included in his indictment the "folk-fakery" of Broadway musicals and the more general middlebrow "nostalgia for small-town life." Wood's sometimes ponderous claims about regionalist art—that it had freed American painting from colonialism and the ivory tower—invited critics as early as 1935 to attack *American Gothic* for its midcult anti-aesthetic. Wood's "very cleverly conceived double portrait of a farmer and his wife," one wrote, "immediately won the affections of hundreds of earnest exhibition-goers who suffered an inferiority complex when confronted with more complex art forms."[117]

After his death, a memorial exhibition at the Art Institute unleashed a series of critical attacks that the *Art Digest* summed up as "Knocking Wood" or, less cleverly, "The Grant Wood Controversy." While some grudgingly acknowledged that *American Gothic* was a "real achievement," these critics agreed that most of his paintings were emotionally and intellectually vapid. Wood, Dorothy Odenheimer wrote in the *Chicago Sun*, "was a provincial whose vision was restricted in more than a physical sense to the rolling hills of Iowa. He had no taste, no sense of color, no feeling for texture." His paintings, in the terms by which critics damned middlebrow art, were "manufactured according to a pattern"—a crowd-pleasing "formula" that he found with *American Gothic* and used "over and over again." Only the degraded tastes of the American public—its preference for "slick painting, clean-cut lines and smooth surfaces"—could account for the enormous popularity of a painter who, according to another critic, knew less about art, "technically and creatively, than hundreds of illustrators whose work adorns the slick paper magazines." Wood was guilty of producing "mass-appeal art," a scholar from the University of Wisconsin complained in the magazine *Art in America*. Like other purveyors of midcult, he was "content to dwell on extra-aesthetic delights of immediate recognition"—that is, his middlebrow admirers could bypass any difficult considerations of form and easily understand the content of his paintings. The "more discriminating spectator" could discern that his work identified "democracy with mediocrity" by exchanging standards for popularity.[118]

Even C. J. Bulliet, the Chicago critic who took credit for "starting the vogue for Grant Wood" with his praise for *American Gothic*, now accused Wood of having little more than "a shrewd sense of showmanship and a sort of pictorial demagoguery"—a dangerous masscult/midcult tendency to pander to rather than challenge popular expectations. *American Gothic*, though still his best painting, was "small-souled." (Bulliet, according to Nan Wood Graham, turned on her brother because of a personal grudge. Wood had served on an Art Institute jury that rejected a painting by Bulliet's "lady friend." An infuriated Bulliet "let loose a vitriolic attack" and "continued to say vicious things about Grant, as did his parrot followers," after Wood's death.)[119]

Beyond its aesthetic weaknesses—"Note the tiresome repetition of dots and circles on the apron of the woman in 'American Gothic,'" said Fritzi Weisenborn in the *Chicago Times*—Wood's work struck critics during and after the war as politically retrograde. It was, Weisenborn proclaimed, "isolationist"; Wood had "shouted that all foreigners and European art were decadent and that we must isolate ourselves completely." This made him popular during the Depression, observed Peyton Boswell in *Art Digest*, when "the U. S. thought-trend was nationalistic in complexion." But no longer—not with the United States "forced by fascist enemies into an all-out war for the democratic way of living." In this "global struggle" where "a defeat for Britain" was "a defeat for us" and "a victory for Russia" was "a victory for us" (and the democratic way of living?), Boswell concluded, "Flag waving has become something of a felony." With internationalism in the ascendant, Wood's "rugged nationalism" was "in eclipse." His images of homely Americans cocooned by their barns, fields, trees, and fences, ignorant of what was happening beyond their farms and towns, belonged already to the bankrupt past.

Wood's "importance died with the decade of the 30's," Odenheimer wrote, while Weisenborn, insisting that "art is never national but always international in intent and content," issued an even more emphatic dismissal: "Grant Wood's work which hangs in the gallery of honor at the Art Institute contributes nothing scientifically, emotionally, or esthetically to art or society. It is the culmination of a trend of escapist and isolationist thought which was popular with some groups yesterday, but which is definitely obsolete today."[120] Drafted by *Fortune* to help fight the war in 1941, *American Gothic* struck critics a year later as an emblem of the head-in-the-sand attitudes that had brought the war about.

In a scathing scholarly assessment of Wood's work in 1943, H. W. Janson, a refugee from Nazi Germany, directly linked Wood's middlebrow "anti-artistic" ethos to its "dangerous" political implications. Wood's "sales appeal," Janson argued, had everything to do with the substitution of "'Americanism,' i.e. nationalism, for esthetic values of any kind": with a perverse insistence that subject matter—and an extremely limited subject matter at that—was the sole determinant of a painting's merit. For a painting "to be truly American," according to this credo, it "must show an American farm scene in plainly recognizable fashion, since cities are polluted by alien influences." Janson perceptively located the sources of Wood's "amazing popularity" during the 1930s:

> In a period of economic and political crisis he placed
> before the public a vision of stability and security,
> untouched by the depression or by the disquieting
> events abroad that were beginning to cast their shad-
> ows over this country. Nor is it surprising that his work
> should have appealed so tremendously to the urban
> population, whose need for a "substitute reality" was
> greatest.

This reassuring isolationism, this insidious promulgation
of "the fiction of our economic and cultural self-sufficiency,"
driven by regionalism's "ruthless sales technique" (compara-
ble to those other bastions of midcult, the bestseller publish-
ers and Hollywood), wasn't much different from the cultural
politics of the Nazis. "Little wonder," Janson wrote, "that
Grant Wood's style should prove to be so similar to some of the
artistic developments accompanying the rise of nationalism in
Europe since the late 1920's": the celebration of "healthy"
native art versus "degenerate" foreign art; the denigration of
corrupt urban life in favor of "the idyllic aspects of rural and
small-town life"; the strict insistence on "pure and simple"
pictorial representation against formal experimentation and
difficulty. "In fact, almost every one of the ideas constituting
the regionalist credo could be matched more or less verbatim
from the writings of Nazi experts on art," he concluded. (Janson, an art historian teaching at Washington University during World War II, went on to write the popular and influential
textbook *History of Art*, first published in 1962, which, not
surprisingly, made no mention of Wood in its chapter on

twentieth-century painting. A few lines on regionalism, without naming Benton, Curry, or Wood, were added in the third edition in 1986.)[121]

The battle between nationalism—whether it took the form of a resurgent isolationism or an imperialist aggressiveness à la Henry Luce's "American Century"—and internationalism was being waged in the field of art as well as politics, and the outcome of "the Grant Wood controversy," according to these critics, would be of much more than art historical significance. The man with the pitchfork was engaged in a reactionary defense of the discredited aesthetics and politics of the 1930s.

But alongside these larger aesthetic and political concerns, the hostility of postwar intellectuals to midcult had a lot to do with the stubborn refusal of the middlebrows to heed their ministrations. In the culture wars of the 1940s and 1950s, both sides linked the art they liked to freedom and the art they loathed to totalitarianism. Wood's most outspoken defender, Thomas Craven, fretted at the beginning of World War II about the "moral softening" of American society at the hands of the un-American types who controlled the art world. These "puny men, some of them weaklings, others inverted," influenced "the young to scorn all native artists who perform with originality and a knowledge of American values." (*Newsweek* described Craven in 1943 as the critic "best liked by the reading public and most disliked by the art world.") The nation's middlebrow-in-chief, Harry Truman, confided in his diary that the Old Masters were to "the lazy, nutty moderns" as Christ was to Lenin. The red-baiting Michigan congressman George Dondero took to the House floor to denounce "all the isms"—culminating in "abstractionism"—that were "stabbing our glorious American art in the back with murderous intent." Invoking the authority of Craven, Dondero scoffed at those "with only a superficial knowledge of the complicated influences that surge in the art world of today" who insisted that modern art wasn't Communist because the Soviets officially hated it too. With his deeper knowledge, Dondero could say definitively that abstractionism and Communism were one and the same, and that a "horde of germ-carrying art vermin" ("the effeminate elect" that Craven and Benton also abhorred) were threatening the nation with "depravity, decadence, and destruction." Truman's less virulent complaints about modern "monstrosities" sounded more like Babbitt than Goebbels and probably reflected the more common view. "Any kid can take an egg and a piece of ham and make more understandable pictures," he wrote. Unlike Dondero, he didn't claim to be an expert, but he knew what made "real art appealing." It was "beautiful and heart warming."[122]

In the case of Wood—and *American Gothic* especially— the middlebrows simply ignored the critics' claim that he and it were obsolete. Sales of *American Gothic* reproductions went "marching on" during World War II, Craven happily observed in the *Saturday Evening Post*, and it continued to be "the most popular American painting since Whistler's Mother." Indignant letter-writers rallied to Wood's defense against the highbrows. "I would resent any one telling me what brand of tobacco to smoke and what beer to drink. I resent as much any loudmouthed commentator on art telling me what I should admire and what to abhor," a Virginia man wrote to the *Art Digest*, whose editors themselves defended Wood against the "wrath of the international ivory-towerists" and called *American Gothic* indisputably "one of the great pictures of the twentieth century." At the opening of the Art Institute's memorial exhibit, the lieutenant governor of Iowa prophesied that Wood's paintings would "live so long as the rugged virtues of a vigorous free America are remembered." *Time*, *Life*, and *Newsweek* were equally kind in their eulogies. *Life* featured a seven-page color spread in conjunction with the show, including a photo of Nan and Dr. McKeeby posed in front of *American Gothic*, and told its readers that "a neighboring farmer's approval of one of his pictures meant more to Wood than all the acclaim"—and

Nan Wood Graham and Byron McKeeby pose together for the first time at the Art Institute of Chicago in 1942. They posed separately for American Gothic *in 1930. [Unknown Photographer,* Nan Wood Graham and Dr. B.H. McKeeby at the Art Institute of Chicago, 1942. *From the Cedar Rapids Museum of Art Archives.]*

presumably the ire—"of worldly art critics."[123]

In 1949, with Wood's reputation among such critics in precipitous decline, *Life* ran an article titled "High-Brow, Low-Brow, Middle-Brow," based on a piece in *Harper's* by the self-described "upper middlebrow" journalist Russell Lynes. In the photograph introducing the article, three men stand, their backs to the camera, "in clothes characteristic of their cultural stations," looking at the pictures they like. "One, a tall man in a baggy tweed suit, likes paintings by Picasso. The next, a man in shirtsleeves, enjoys calendar art. The third likes Grant Wood reproductions suitable for framing"—*American Gothic* in the photo. "The first is a high-brow, the second a low-brow, the third a middle-brow." *Life* delighted in

American Gothic *as the epitome of middlebrow culture in 1949.* [Life]

explaining that "The high-brow would like to get rid of the middle-brow, but the middle-brow outnumbers him."[124]

Ten years later, *American Gothic* was advertised as one of five "priceless paintings you can afford" which, through a remarkable new process called "color separation," made it "possible to mass-produce fine works of art with such fidelity that at 20 feet it's sometimes hard to tell the difference between the original painting and the photographic copy" and thus to hang a "gallery of great art . . . in your own home at a fraction of its original cost." The announcements of *American Gothic*'s death were premature; it lived on, as *Life* and *The Music Man* revealed, in the mass-produced middlebrow culture that so many postwar intellectuals deplored.[125]

I first saw *American Gothic* in 1960s advertisements: in a General Mills Country Corn Flakes commercial or maybe even on an actual box of Country Corn Flakes, bought by my mother in one of many attempts to give a healthier start to our days and undoubtedly rejected by my brother and me in favor of the space-age sweetness of Jets or Quisp. Unlike the outraged Cedar Rapids folks who found the use of *American Gothic* to advertise cereal "disgusting, repulsive, and loathsome"—it "flagrantly prostitutes a piece of art by our own Grant Wood"—I'm sure I didn't switch off the TV when the commercial came on. It wasn't the marketing strategy I found "revolting," and I certainly didn't care, as the Ohio State University art historian Matthew Baigell did, that the commercial reinforced the Wood-haters' complaint that his art was "corny." Baigell introduced his 1966 article "Grant Wood Revisited," which tried to rescue Wood's work from the purgatory of kitsch, by describing the commercial and calling it a "pity" that one of Wood's most "acid" paintings had been "so closely associated with corn of one sort or another for so many years." The corn flakes-*American Gothic* connection probably succeeded in signaling "wholesome" to me. I just preferred much more sugar in my cereal.[126]

The Country Corn Flakes commercial was produced in 1963 after an earlier commercial, featuring the Scarecrow from *The Wizard of Oz*, had the upsetting effect, from General Mills's perspective, of boosting sales of *Kellogg's* Corn Flakes. Len Glasser, who wrote and directed the *American Gothic* spot (and earned profits on it of only $1,200, even though it was one of the highest-rated and longest-running commercials in TV history), says that the idea of using the image came easily. Glasser had named his company, which was commissioned to do the commercial by the advertising agency Dancer Fitzgerald Sample, "Stars & Stripes Productions Forever" to capitalize on the fact that "Americana was becoming very hip in advertising at that time." Using actors to play the *American Gothic* figures, Glasser intercut live action with animation ("crazy stuff" like farm animals spit-roasting boxes of cereal). The actors lip-synched a song that Glasser wrote to the chord changes of "You Are My Sunshine," actually sung by the Weavers (he'd wanted the Smothers Brothers), praising the virtues of Country Corn Flakes. At one point, the woman joined the man in looking directly at the camera and singing, "Please buy our corn flakes." An animation website calls it "quite possibly the most subversive cereal commercial ever made"—an example of the new "hip" advertising that sold products to knowing consumers by making fun of advertising itself.[127]

   American Gothic also made its sitcom debut in 1963, on an episode of *The Dick Van Dyke Show*. Rob and Laura Petrie (Dick Van Dyke and Mary Tyler Moore) think they're the owners of an original parody of *American Gothic*—of a lost variation by Grant Wood himself that they've discovered under an ugly clown portrait they accidentally bought at an auction:

> *Rob:* Honey, it's the same people. It's the same house as in *American Gothic*. It's even the same pitchfork!
>
> *Laura:* Yeah, but our people are smiling.
>
> *Rob:* Well, maybe they had a good crop that year. You know, in the famous one, maybe they could have just found out they had worms in their tomatoes or something.

Further convinced of their good luck when they expose the "ood" part of the signature, they are disappointed to learn from an expert that their *American Gothic* is really a Nathaniel Good, a bad imitator of Grant Wood. The writers needed a painting that would be instantly recognizable to an American sitcom audience. The episode was titled "The Masterpiece."[128]

   The second place I saw *American Gothic* was on a different sitcom: at the end of the opening credits on *Green Acres*. That theme song still occupies a part of my brain that could have been put to more productive uses, and even though I hadn't watched the show in years until I viewed the first episode for "research" at the Museum of Television and Radio, I knew exactly what was coming when Oliver Wendell

Douglas (Eddie Albert) sang to his wife Lisa (Eva Gabor), "You are my wife," and she resignedly replied "Goodbye city life." They would end the credits standing in front of their ramshackle farm house in Hooterville, posed like those old-timey farmers who advertised corn flakes, and he would stamp the soil with the handle of his pitchfork in unison with the theme song's emphatic last two notes.

Green Acres is a show that manages to be exceedingly stupid even as it devastatingly sends up American agrarian myths. Oliver, we learn in the first episode, is an unhappy Manhattan lawyer, forced into this career by his father despite his pleas to be a farmer (which we hear and see in a news report–style flash-back, narrated by *What's My Line* host John Daly). "My roots are in the soil," he tells the befuddled Lisa, who can only answer, "So that's what you want to do: soil your roots." Oliver's mother points out that he was born on a farm by accident—the family was vacationing in Saratoga Springs—and lived there for only two days. But Oliver is fixated on the idea of returning to the land—reading USDA publications on his lunch hour, trying to grow corn on his penthouse terrace—and on a business trip to Chicago (with a stop at the Art Institute?), he takes a long detour to Hooterville to buy "the Haney place."

It is in the scene in Sam Drucker's general store in Hooter-ville that we learn the premise of the show's entire six-season run from 1965 to 1971: that Oliver is more ridiculous than the hicks he comes to live among. Arnold the pig guffaws when he hears that Mr. Haney has sold his rundown farm to the city lawyer. The denizens of Drucker's store are understandably perplexed by Oliver's Jeffersonian paean to agrarian life. He has moved to Hooterville "to join hands with you the farmers, the backbone of our economy." The anchorman, equally perplexed, begins his report by explaining, "In 1930, there were over 32 million people living on farms. In the thirty-five years that followed, more than 20 million sold their farms and moved to the city. To the best of my knowledge, in this same period of time, only one man got rid of his Park Avenue penthouse and bought a farm." Oliver has been taken in by *American Gothic*'s image of rural wholesomeness, authenticity, and self-sufficiency. If, as the sitcom historian Gerard Jones observes, Oliver finds himself "at sea in the irrational American heartland," he is no less irrational for believing that he will find a Grant Wood pastoral any place other than in a painting.[129]

The creator of *Green Acres*, Paul Henning, was also responsible for *The Beverly Hillbillies*, another sitcom that intersected with *American Gothic*. In February 1963, a couple of months into the *Hillbillies*' run, the cover of the *Saturday Evening Post* featured the lead characters in the *American Gothic* pose, with Jed Clampett holding the pitchfork and Granny wearing the rickrack apron and the cameo. Though *Green Acres* would reverse the situation—urbanites transplanted among bumpkins rather than bumpkins transplanted among urbanites—the gist of the pose seems to be the same for both shows: Rural folk are backward to the point of zaniness. The Clampett clan's misadventures in the consumer economy constitute the organizing joke of *The Beverly Hillbillies*. As millionaires, they are supposed to consume fully and freely, yet they inevitably get it wrong. Gerard Jones sums up the show's typical gags: "Jed sees his vast new lawn and wants to plow it for crops; Granny tries to find possum innards in L.A. stores for her down-home 'vittles'; Jed thinks 'golf' is some sort of game animal and mistakes the balls for eggs."[130]

But if the *Hillbillies* indicates on one hand "that there's

just no place for provincials in mainstream culture," Jones
remarks, it also suggests "that we can preserve simple values in the modern world." Born in Missouri, Henning portrayed his transplanted rural folk as innocents. Underlying
the zaniness, notes the critic David Marc, the show's theme
is "the conflict between middle-American virtue and Los
Angeles decadence." In April 1968 (like *Green Acres*, the
Hillbillies went on until 1971), *TV Guide* ran a story about
Irene Ryan, the actress who played Granny, titled "American Gothic On Television and Off." The story referred back
to the *Post* cover and observed that "if one were to boil
[Ryan] down to a single visual image, one could end up
with the feminine half of Grant Wood's 'American Gothic'—
that famous painting of a tough, disciplined, morally rigor-
ous old Iowa couple." Ryan herself invoked the image to
criticize student protests and the welfare state ("They're
putting everybody on the dole. It absolutely ruins ambition
in people"):

> Like most other people who have the "American
> Gothic" character, Irene Ryan has decidedly mixed
> feelings about the contemporary scene. Some aspects
> of 20th-century America—the pioneering, adventur-
> ous aspects—excite her. "There's no place on earth
> like America," she says. "We've advanced in so many
> wonderful ways—in architecture, in science, in
> space. I'm sorry I'm as old as I am. I'd like to live
> another hundred years. The moon! I'd like to *see* the
> damn thing."
>
> But she's less than excited about the younger
> generation. "They lack discipline. On the set, for

example, it's Buddy Ebsen (Jed Clampett) and I who
have the discipline. Max Baer (Jethro) and Donna
Douglas (Ellie Mae)—they're the ones who are late
and seldom apologize for it, seldom call. I wouldn't
think of coming in late. And take these protesters. I
don't like the manner in which they protest. Anybody
has a right to protest, but you've got to go about it in
the right way—not kick in cars and hurt people. It's
lack of discipline."

Ryan told Nan Wood Graham that the *Post* cover, on display in
her den, was her "most treasured possession" and conveyed
her hope that "the Hillbillies are a tribute to your brother's
painting."[131]

Parody here is transformed into homage—homage not
only to the original image on which the parody is based but to
the "original" message of that image. *Green Acres* used a parody of *American Gothic* to send up the notion that rural Americans still have a privileged claim to represent the nation. Yet
Ryan and *TV Guide* continued to associate *American Gothic*
with "the essence of the American character": with those values invoked by Ryan—the pioneer spirit, progress, toughness,
self-discipline, moral rigor—that supposedly constitute "our
national identity."[132]

Parody was a signature mode of
the 1960s—a vital component of an emerging postmodern sensibility that delighted in the endless recycling of texts and
images, in playful "quotation" and self-referentiality, in col-

lapsing distinctions between high and low culture, between the serious and the frivolous. It was the mode of Andy Warhol's Brillo boxes and Campbell's Soup cans and Roy Lichtenstein's comic-strip canvases, of Vaughn Meader's impersonations of John Kennedy and Rich Little's and David Frye's of Richard Nixon, of *MAD* magazine (which in 1970 illustrated a parody called *Silent Majority: The Magazine for Middle America* by placing a smiling Nixon between the *American Gothic* couple, his hands on their shoulders), of the metafictional games with traditional literary forms in John Barth's and Thomas Pynchon's novels, of *The Monkees* and Rowan and Martin's *Laugh-In*. Susan Sontag's influential essays of the early 1960s celebrated parody as "a flight from interpretation," from the "reactionary, stifling," impoverishing, depleting "idea that a work of art is primarily its content." Pop Art, with its replications of the products of mass culture, used content "so blatant, so 'what it is,'" Sontag wrote approvingly, that it made any appeal to "the intellect at the expense of energy and sensual capability" impossible. Many of the decade's parodies represented a Merry Prankster attitude toward conventions, traditions, authorities, and icons. Some ridiculed the images or texts they parodied. But others didn't. Parody, the theorist Linda Hutcheon maintains, frequently combines "respectful homage and ironically thumbed nose." *American Gothic* was more often a weapon than a target in its proliferating parodies.[133]

Almost all of the *American Gothic* parodies—from presidents and first ladies to Mickey and Minnie Mouse, hippies to yuppies, ads for consumer electronics to editorial cartoons about farm foreclosures, women's libbers to Ken and Barbie—operate with the same basic conceit. They manipulate the details of the original, usually the faces, often the clothing,

Richard Nixon cozies up to middle America, the "silent majority," in a 1970 Mad magazine parody. [From MAD #139 © 1970 E.C. Publications, Inc. All rights reserved. Used with permission.]

Barbie and Ken meet American Gothic on a Hallmark anniversary card. [BARBIE® and KEN® are trademarks owned by and used with permission from Mattel, Inc. © 2005 Mattel, Inc. All rights reserved. © Hallmark Licensing, Inc., 1997. Reprinted with permission.]

sometimes the pitchfork or the house, either to signify the differences between the "then" of the painting and the now of the parody or to collapse those differences—or, most often, to do both at once.

In 1961, S&H Green Stamps ran an advertisement titled "Who changed the picture of the farmer's wife?" A young woman, Mrs. Luke Oberwise Jr. of Harvard, Illinois, stands in front of *American Gothic*. Her sharp New Look hairdo, hat, and dress, including a chic gold collar pin, set her off from the old-fashioned rickracked and brooched woman (a "farmer's wife" again!) in the painting. We learn that her standard of living is nearly double that of her predecessor's, that she is "no longer chained to the chunk stove—and her hands show it" (she holds a book), she is better educated, "no longer isolated from people and ideas," much more interested in art, music, and drama, sufficiently freed from drudgery to find time "to channel her energy into new and better ways to help her family." One of these ways, of course, is to collect Green Stamps. *American Gothic* highlights the distance that "the average farm wife" has traveled in becoming virtually indistinguishable from the other beneficiaries of Cold War prosperity and domesticity. But it also helps market Green Stamps by homage rather than juxtaposition. Clearly, the figures in *American Gothic* embody the "American Way of Thrift" that Green Stamps took as its slogan, and "being thrifty," the ad reminded careful consumers, "will never be old-fashioned"—even though the whole idea behind Green Stamps was to encourage saving through spending for purposes of future spending. The Cold War redefined freedom and democracy as consumer choice: the American Way of Life. "To us, diversity, the right to choose," Vice President Richard Nixon told Soviet Premier

The farmer's wife has come a long way, but she still practices the traditional virtues of thrift in this 1961 advertisement for S&H Green Stamps. [The Sperry and Hutchinson Company, Inc.]

Nikita Khrushchev during the famous "Kitchen Debate" at a display of American home appliances in Moscow in 1959, "is the most important thing." The Green Stamps ad reinforced the patriotism of consumption by linking "modern" and "old-fashioned" American values. It located *American Gothic* in the past only to end up invoking its timelessness.[134]

Though not itself a parody, "Who changed the picture of the farmer's wife?" inaugurated what we might call the "lifestyle" subgenre of *American Gothic* parodies. "Look how far we've come!" these parodies exclaim as they adorn the figures in the painting with the accoutrements of abundance and leisure: preppy attire, evening wear, sunglasses, hors d'oeuvres, tennis rackets and golf clubs, fishing rods, scuba gear, consumer electronics, luxury cars. Those poor self-denying folks, the juxtapositions suggest, had cramped lives; we have fulfilling lifestyles. This is a curious twist given that leftist critics blasted Wood during the Depression for making his farms and farmers, towns and townspeople look *too* prosperous. But it also recalls the early response of fun-loving moderns to the image's fun-loathing Puritans. No doubt there's a chuckle in the inauthenticity of Paul Newman and his daughter posed à la *American Gothic* on the packaging for his brand of organic snack foods. The image of a movie star pretending to be down-to-earth in marketing pretzels or peanut-butter cups exhibits a playful ironic distance, to say the least. The company's slogan, after all, is "Shameless Exploitation in Pursuit of the Common Good." Yet such an image also supports the company's reputation for purity: Its products are "nutritious" and "all-natural," and its profits are donated to charity. Unlike the Country Corn Flakes of my childhood, Newman's Own Organics have won me over with their claim of wholesomeness.[135]

Instead of disparaging the "original," *American Gothic* parodies frequently use it as a standard for evaluating contemporary society and politics. Sometimes the contemporary doesn't measure up to what *TV Guide* called the "American Gothic hard core" of national character. But often, because of the association with *American Gothic*, it defies appearances and turns out to preserve that hard core after all. When *American Heritage* ran a story a few years ago about divorce—one of those contemporary phenomena that indicated to many an erosion of character—the magazine put *American Gothic* on the cover and split the "couple" by shooting a jagged white line, like a lightning bolt, through the center of the image. Divorce, the article insisted, is not a departure from the American heritage but a "national institution," rooted in "a continent's imperatives and a people's love of independence and infatuation with individualism"—a sign, it turns out, of constancy in the American character, "of our fervent belief in love and marriage," in "a happy marriage" as "every individual's birthright." Readers of the article objected less to its recasting of divorce as entirely compatible with traditional American "family values" than to the cover's suggestion that *American Gothic* depicts a husband and wife instead of a father and daughter. "We could hardly have gotten more letters if we'd identified Emmanuel Leutze's best-known painting as *Jefferson Crossing the Delaware*," the editors quipped as they explained that there has never been a consensus on the figures' relationship.[136]

Alfred Gescheidt, the most accomplished *American Gothic* parodist, was among the first to plug the faces of presidential couples into the image. Starting in the sixties with Lyndon and Lady Bird Johnson, he and others have parodied every president and first lady since. Gescheidt has never used computers; he looks carefully through photo archives to choose the images that will fit best, then cuts, pastes, and retouches by hand. He considers what he does an homage to the painting ("I happen to love Grant Wood's work") rather than a political intervention ("I don't

Alfred Gescheidt has parodied almost every presidential couple since Lady Bird and Lyndon Johnson. [Photograph © Alfred Gescheidt]

Gescheidt also helped introduce the "strange bedfellows" subgenre of American Gothic parodies with the African American New York Congress-woman Shirley Chisholm and the segregationist Alabama Governor George Wallace, both Democratic presidential candidates in 1972. [Photograph © Alfred Gescheidt]

Nancy and Ronald Reagan by Alfred Gescheidt. [Photograph © Alfred Gescheidt] even think about it verbally"), though he doesn't conceal his particular dislike of Republicans. For his most successful parody—the one of the Reagans, which sold millions of copies as postcards and T-shirts—he spent half a day rummaging through Nancy and Ronald photos, until he finally found the "shit-eating expressions" he was looking for.[137]

What happens when presidential couples are *American Gothic*ized? One effect is to raise questions about the relationship between president and electorate by lampooning the "just folks" roles that seem necessary for winning the office and performing it publicly. However humble the president's origins may be, these parodies suggest, the distance between the folksy performances and the realities of the imperial pres-

The Carters being "just folks" amid the trappings of the imperial presidency. [Mike Peters, Dayton Daily News, *1977. Library of Congress, Prints & Photographs Division, Cartoon Drawings Collection, reproduction number LC-USZ62-126431.]*

idency is enormous. A 1977 cartoon marks the distance explicitly by posing Rosalynn and Jimmy Carter, recently arrived in Washington from Plains, Georgia, in *American Gothic* dress in front of the White House. Flanking the smiling first lady and the beaming, toothsome president on the back lawn are a presidential limousine and helicopter, each accompanied by a line of military officials standing at attention, waiting for the couple to turn away from the viewer, enter the White House, hand off the pitchfork to an aide, get out of the apron and overalls, and get down to the real business of power. The joke is about representation: Representing the first couple as the *American Gothic* couple hints at the dubiousness of the presidency's claim to represent the "middle America" that represents the nation.[138]

For the *Los Angeles Times* editorial cartoonist Paul Conrad, the hold of "middle America" over national politics has been the subject of a series of *American Gothic* parodies since the fifties. A 1954 Conrad cartoon replaced the couple's heads with the Democratic donkey and the Republican elephant and skewered Dwight Eisenhower on the pitchfork, no match for the bipartisan congressional opposition to reducing farm price supports. A 1964 cartoon featured the pitchfork-wielding man, standing for "rural-dominated state legislatures," lashing out at the flustered woman, "reapportionment" written across her apron, who along with the Supreme Court has been nagging him about fairness in political representation: one man, one vote. A 1970 cartoon turned the man into a cigar-smoking fat cat and the woman into his fur-draped mistress or trophy wife, again to criticize the federal government's enormous crop subsidy program.

More commonly, *American Gothic* has been pressed into

"Nag, nag, nag!...that's all you and the U. S. Supreme Court ever do...!!!"

American Gothic *has been a staple for* Los Angeles Times *editorial cartoonist Paul Conrad, who has used it to weigh in on issues ranging from crop subsidies to the gender gap in voting. [Paul Conrad. Copyright, Tribune Media Services, Inc. All rights reserved. Reprinted with permission.]*

American Gothic—1970

"TAKE OFF THAT STUPID BUTTON!"

political service to locate a position or movement in the national mainstream—to counter the "silent majority" conservatism of the couple superimposed on an American flag under the exhortation "God Bless America and Please Hurry." A 1973 parody put a smile on the woman's face, an "ERA Yes" sign in her hand, and the U.S. Capitol building behind her and her partner. Later in the decade, an anti-nuclear parody turned their faces into skulls above the word "Meltdown!" There is a risk, though, in using *American Gothic* to promote a more inclusive Americanism. Since the "original" must remain present for the parody to work, this presence always threatens to undermine the ostensible inclusiveness of the parody. The authenticity of the "original"—the assumption of a stable iconic meaning that most of the parodies depend on— implies the inauthenticity of the parody's stand-ins.[139]

The countercultural parodies of the late 1960s and 1970s shared with their less outrageous counterparts this understanding of what *American Gothic* represents. The difference was that they used the image much more explicitly to mock "middle America." A 1967 poster put peace signs in the pattern of the woman's apron and a daffodil in her hand, swapped her brooch for a German iron cross, pinned a "Flower Power" button on the man's lapel, replaced the pitchfork with an "Up the Establishment" placard, and stuck a banana in his other hand (labeled "Mello," an indication that he intends to smoke it for the high that bananas were rumored to produce).[140] The shadow of a police helicopter on the roof and across the gothic window portends a raid in Gilbert Shelton and Dave Sheridan's version of *American Gothic* on the cover of a *Fabulous Furry Freak Brothers* comic book, titled "Grass Roots," in 1977. The couple and the photographer taking their picture (perhaps hallucinogens heightened reality to the point where *American Gothic*

The countercultural American Gothic. *She has peace signs on her apron.*
He wears a flower power button and holds a banana—supposedly a source of
a cheap and legal high. [Personality Posters, Inc. Library of Congress,
Prints & Photographs Division, Yanker Poster Collection, video frame ID
LCPP001A-38836]

seemed more like a photograph than a painting) look up in alarm as other members of their pot- and mushroom-producing collective flee naked into the marijuana fields. The lifestyle parodies that sell products by contrasting cool consumers with the uncool figures in the "original" derive from these counter-cultural parodies. Since the late 1960s, it has been much easier to be ironic about the "original" image than to see the image as ironic.

Gescheidt was pleased that Nan Wood Graham complimented him at the opening of a retrospective of her brother's work, which included a display of parodies, at the Whitney Museum in New York in 1983. He'd heard that if she didn't like his work, she'd sue. Nan had, in fact, filed a lawsuit against Johnny Carson and *Look* and *Playboy* magazines in May 1968, just after *TV Guide*'s homage to her brother's painting prompted her to exchange fond letters with Irene Ryan. In a *Tonight Show* bit that *Look* dubbed "make-fun-of-the-classics time—an old routine, but Carson does it well," Johnny held up a version of *American Gothic* in which the man is topless and the woman nearly so, with a low-riding bikini barely covering her breasts. *Look* included a photo of the scene in a Carson profile in July 1967. The following October, the letters section of *Playboy* featured a parody that went a step further than what late-night TV could get away with. Kelly Riordan of Champaign, Illinois, had grafted onto the *American Gothic* woman the torso of May 1966 play-

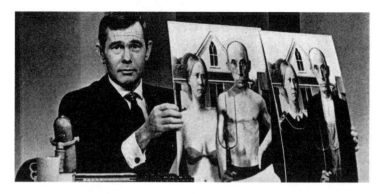

Little did Johnny Carson know that "make-fun-of-the-classics time" on the Tonight Show *would get him sued by Nan Wood Graham. [Photo by Philippe Halsman © Halsman Estate]*

mate Dolly Read, her arm provocatively stretched behind the woman's head, her purple turtleneck pulled above her exposed breasts. *Playboy*'s editors called it a "nice combination of the traditional and the contemporary" and hoped that Dolly Read wouldn't "object to being de-faced." Their facetious worries were misdirected: The objection didn't come from the de-faced playmate but from the re-bodied Nan.[141]

Nan and her lawyers based her nine-million-dollar suit on the "well-known fact that I am the woman in the painting 'American Gothic,' " as she put it in her answer to the defense attorney's questions. (In 1970, Nan appeared on the CBS quiz show *To Tell the Truth.* The show's premise was that the celebrity panelists—Bennett Cerf, Peggy Cass, Bill Cullen, and Kitty Carlisle—had to guess which of three contestants really was the woman in the painting. Only Carlisle guessed correctly. Nan took home $250 for each of the three incorrect votes.) The parodies, the suit claimed, were "vile and obscene," "false, untrue, libelous and defamatory," and had brought "contempt and ridicule" upon her. She was "shocked and stunned" when she saw them, Nan recounted in *Newsweek*, and was equally distressed by the obscene phone calls she received at home in Riverside, California. "Who wouldn't be upset?" she asked in *Time*. "People think I posed for the terrible picture they made of it. I was ashamed to go to church for a month." One wry letter to the editor suggested that "If some people really think that Nan Wood Graham posed for the bikini and topless versions, she should be happy to pay $9 million to Johnny Carson and *Playboy* in appreciation." *Newsweek* must have upset her further by referring to the couple in the painting as "an austere bespectacled Midwestern farmer and his tight-lipped, gastralgic wife." But she was cheered by other letters that called *American Gothic* "a treasure and not something for ridicule," and by predictions that her suit would put an end to the "gamier" spoofs.[142]

As the press accounts of the *Tonight Show-Playboy* lawsuit pointed out, Nan didn't object to the milder takeoffs. "I get a kick out of it when it is done in good taste," she said, and she proudly displayed a collection of them on a wall of her bungalow. One of the earliest, dating back long before the proliferation of *American Gothic*ana in the 1960s, was her own painting *The Three of Us*, done a few months after her brother's death, in which she superimposed between and slightly below her and Dr. McKeeby "a cherub-faced Grant," his "angelic countenance," as the *Cedar Rapids Gazette* reported, punctuated by the "tiny horns" formed by two prongs of the pitchfork. The defendants' lawyers made a point of bringing up *The Three of Us*, but Nan rightly responded that hers was a "far cry" from the offending images. The *Tonight Show* and *Playboy* parodies, she felt, unquestionably crossed the line from tribute to desecration.[143]

The irony is that these desecrations assumed precisely the "original" *American Gothic* that Nan cherished: the wholesome, unironic version that had come into existence during the Depression and World War II. Taking the clothes off the figures in the late 1960s—at the height of the sexual revolution—was a knock on the Puritanism of middle America, but it also fixed the image as a representation of the "earnest, hard-working, don't-tread-on-me types" that Nan saw in her brother's painting. She won a small settlement, but it's doubtful that "by just being filed and getting such big publicity all over the country" her lawsuit made future parodists "think twice before desecrating" *American Gothic*. Just a few years later, in 1977, she sued *Hustler* for ten million dollars for another naked send-up; this time she lost. ("You'd Be Sour, Too, If You Were Subject of Countless Spoofs," read a *Wall Street Journal* front-page headline after the *Hustler* suit was thrown out.)[144]

Nan died in 1990 and was spared seeing *American Gothic* used to advertise the 2003 Fox-TV "reality" show *The Simple Life*, in which celebrity party girls Paris Hilton and Nicole Richie are forced to live on an Arkansas farm. In the ads, Paris wears a denim bustier and holds a chihuahua; Nicole wears unclasped overalls and a bikini and holds a pitchfork. Nan might have taken comfort, though, in learning that fans of her brother's painting again complained that the ads debased it. A Fox spokesman responded by noting that the people who posed for *American Gothic* weren't really farm folk either. "They are symbols of American down-to-earth toughness," he said, "but they would probably have had as much trouble in the rural world as Paris and Nicole. The lesson to remember, with all kinds of celebrity, is it's all illusion, all show business." Despite the executive's efforts to demystify *American Gothic*, Nan might have taken comfort too in the realization that even—especially—the most irreverent (to her, lewd) parodies fortify the "original" as the embodiment of traditional American values. If it can be profaned, it must be sacred.[145]

I n her lawsuits, Nan charged defamation, not copyright infringement. But she did worry that others were increasingly trading on the familiarity of *American Gothic* without compensating her. As the image began to show up even more frequently in the 1970s and 1980s—especially in advertisements and on magazine covers—the issue of who was profiting from it made the question of its copyright status an urgent one. Who owned the rights to *American Gothic*, and what rights did they own? How much could a parody differ from the "original" and still be close enough to require the permission of the rights-holders? And, more broadly, for how long after the death of the actual creator of a work of art—or any other piece of intellectual property —should the work be protected by copyright law? ("The older the work," reasoned Justice Stephen Breyer in a 2003 dissent, "the less likely it is that a sense of authors' rights can justify a copyright holder's decision not to permit reproduction, for the more likely it is that the copyright holder making the decision is not the work's creator, but, say, a corporation or a great-grandchild whom the work's creator never knew.") Whose interests were being served by extending protections for ever longer terms at a time when technologies were making the reproduction and dissemination of texts and images cheaper, easier, and more difficult to control? (The "freezing of the public domain for private benefit," critics have called the effect of these extensions.) When should pieces of "our cultural heritage," as a legal scholar has put it, "be freely available to all to enjoy and to use in creating newer works?"[146]

The copyright status of *American Gothic* is actually a matter of considerable murkiness and disagreement. A 1930 artwork would have remained under its original copyright until 1958. There is no indication in the U.S. Copyright Office's database that Grant Wood or the Art Institute registered the painting in 1930 (not registering an artwork wouldn't have been unusual at that time) or that anyone renewed the copyright in 1958 (which would have been possible even without a 1930 registration). The database does show that Nan registered an *American Gothic* reproduction in March 1952 and that she renewed this registration in 1980. She obviously didn't own the painting, but she probably thought that registering a copy would let her claim rights to the image on the grounds that the copyright didn't pass to the Art Institute when Grant sold the painting in 1930; she would have inherited these rights from him in 1942. A series of revisions to the law—including the "Sonny Bono" Copyright Term Extension Act of 1999, passed under pressure from Disney to prevent the copyright on Mickey Mouse from expiring in 2004—extended valid copyrights on any work produced before 1978 for a total of ninety-five years. Unless Congress acts again to "protect" Mickey, *American Gothic* would enter the public domain in 2025.[147]

In 1988, Nan appointed the Visual Artists and Galleries Association (VAGA) to represent her interests in her brother's work, and the Art Institute and VAGA eventually agreed to share control over rights to *American Gothic*. The Art Institute oversees noncommercial uses of the image. VAGA, which oversees commercial uses, "is known to aggressively pursue infringements, but how it pursues them depends on the nature of the use," says its director, Robert Panzer. Panzer takes an expansive view of what VAGA controls—a view that is far from universally shared. According to Panzer, because no parody can work unless it calls the "original" to viewers' minds, any version of *American Gothic*, no matter how far it strays from the painting in changing clothes, faces, backgrounds, or tools, requires copyright clearance; parodies come under VAGA's authority, he contends, because they always use *American Gothic* to promote something other than an appreciation for or understanding of the painting itself. By the terms of Nan's will, the proceeds from clearances go to the Union Rescue Mission in Los Angeles and to the Riverside County Coalition for Alternatives to Domestic Violence.[148]

VAGA also protects Nan's estate's interests by invoking a legal doctrine known as "right of publicity." California, because of Hollywood, has one of the strongest right-of-publicity laws in the country, and since Nan was a California resident, Panzer reasons, her estate controls the commercial use of her image for seventy years from her death—until 2060. If the right of publicity applies to Nan and *American Gothic* as Panzer says it does, the producers of parodies don't have to know that the woman is her likeness for them to be liable to legal action.[149]

This is a big "if" according to John Busbee, an Iowa arts

journalist who in 2004 explored the "complex web of claims" and raised doubts about their legal merit. Busbee suggested that Nan "had no rights to assign" besides those in the reproduction she registered in 1952, and he questioned whether her heirs could legitimately invoke her publicity right since Nan herself never exercised it. "In the decades old urban myth," he wrote, "a visitor to New York is sold the Brooklyn Bridge. How? Simply because the seller claimed he owned it. Is 'American Gothic' another Brooklyn Bridge?" The only plausible claim to property in *American Gothic*, Busbee argued, is the Art Institute's, and that extends only to the painting and reproductions produced directly from it.[150]

If *American Gothic* comes under the expansive protection that VAGA asserts, then most of the parodies have been illegal, since they were produced and circulated without permission. The Art Institute acknowledged this when in 1976 it refused a request by the VD Hotline in Columbus, Ohio, to use the image in its publicity. Despite his sympathy for the cause—a less moralistic, more open discussion of venereal disease—an Art Institute official explained that he was "in principle opposed to the commercial (advertising) exploitation of works of art, as I am opposed to their mutilation in reproduction, the addition of typeface or 'messages' to their surfaces, etc. Unfortunately," he confessed, "I am often unable to control this misuse, but when I am able I am obliged to do so."[151]

Parody, a more inclusive Americanism, and the threat of legal action came together with niche marketing in the spring of 2000, when Coors, under the leadership of its corporate relations manager for gays and lesbians, Mary Cheney (daughter of conservative cultural commissar Lynne and then soon-to-be vice president Dick), ran an *American Gothic*–themed ad in gay and lesbian publications. In the ad, a very buff young man, shirtless and wearing overalls, holds a pitchfork in one hand and a Coors Light in the other, while a slighter man, whose unbuttoned black shirt and low-necked white T-shirt mimic the blacks and whites of the dress, apron, shirt, and coat of their models, grips the neck of his beer bottle and leans against his companion's shoulder. They appear to be painting their American Gothic house yellow, and they've replaced the peaked window with a less busy rectangle and the patterned curtains with a less stodgy shade or blind. The hook, of course, is that a gay couple has replaced the original "husband and wife" but that in their domesticity, their hard work of making a home, which they cap off with a couple of Coors Lights, they share the values and aspirations of the mainstream.

A viewer of the ad from Fort Smith, Arkansas, criticized it for stereotyping gays in its gestures toward assimilation. "What is particularly offensive is the general misconception that one of the partners in a gay relationship assumes the female role," he wrote. "Hence, the gentleman on the left is showed somewhat limp wristed with an oversized bracelet. Two attractive men doesn't make it real. If you don't understand your market niche, you can't sell to it." Another viewer from Lincoln, Nebraska, was more offended by the "poorly planned" composition. "The guys don't look like a couple, they offer little in respect to the original, and it is a cheap ad," he complained and then advised future commercial parodists: "Don't go messing with an icon unless you have some creative things going on that enhance on the original." The Art Institute and VAGA didn't object to the ad's aesthetic weaknesses or to "messing with an icon" per se. Nor did they object to its depiction of a gay couple. "The gay issue is irrelevant to us," said an Art Institute spokeswoman. But they opposed the image's use in alcohol and tobacco ads, and Coors hadn't asked for permission to parody *American Gothic* in the first place. Nobody pointed out that Jim Beam had reproduced *American Gothic* on a special holiday collector's edition of Beam's Choice Bourbon, part of its Americana series, in 1969. Told to cease and desist, Coors pulled the ad.[152]

With the enormous proliferation of *American Gothic*s, the task of those who represent Wood's estate has been formidable. That proliferation has, in turn, created an *American Gothic* that seems, whether legally or not, to belong to the public domain. Although almost everybody is familiar with the image, many fewer know who painted it. Out of fifty-nine sophomores in the History and Literature program at Harvard whom I surveyed, five correctly identified Wood. All of the students were familiar with the image—thirty-one knew its name—but most were reluctant even to guess at the name of the artist. Nine guessed variously at Homer, Whistler, Hopper, and Rockwell. When my friends posed their twin daughters in an *American Gothic*–style moving announcement and asked "Would you grant us a visit to our new address?" nobody seemed to get the pun. "As the quizzical reactions of the bulk of our friends and family have started to come in," my friend flattered me, "I have been clinging to my fond image of you as the singular person on whom I could count to take enjoyment." *American Gothic* has evolved from the "authored" painting of 1930 (though its meanings were never secured by the intentions of its author) to a work of folk art, quasi-anonymous and of uncertain date (nineteenth century? early twentieth?). [153]

Unlike other icons of the 1930s, it has long since lost its

associations with that time. Tom Joad, as written by John Steinbeck, acted by Henry Fonda, and sung by Woody Guthrie, is indelibly stamped with the Depression. "I'll be ever'where—wherever you look," he famously says. "Wherever they's a fight so hungry people can eat, I'll be there. Wherever they's a cop beatin' up a guy, I'll be there. . . . I'll be in the way guys yell when they're mad an'—I'll be in the way kids laugh when they're hungry an' they know supper's ready. An' when our folks eat the stuff they raise an' live in the houses they build—why, I'll be there." But with *his* lanky figure and overalls, he remains an Everyman figure of a particular time and place. When Bruce Springsteen invoked "the ghost of Tom Joad" in 1995, it was to link contemporary homelessness, unemployment, and migration to the dispossessed of the *Grapes of Wrath* period. Dorothea Lange's *Migrant Mother*, though also occasionally deployed to comment on current injustices, endures as "the canonical image of the Depression," as a historian of photography puts it. For all the transhistorical emotive power of the suffering and perseverance in the wrinkled face of the mother, her children averting the camera and resting their heads on her shoulders, the suffering and perseverance remain grounded in the historical moment of the photograph's production. Even Judy Garland's Dorothy Gale in *The Wizard of Oz*, at least in the Kansas scenes, lives forever amid the black-and-white farmscapes of the Farm Security Administration photographs of the 1930s.[154]

So while mass reproduction and parody have fixed *American Gothic*'s "original" unironic meaning, and while anyone who visits the Art Institute knows who owns the original object, its status as undatable Americana fosters the powerful impression that it is the common property of the nation. How can an unauthored, timeless work be under copyright? That was VAGA's concern when the state committee in charge of choosing the image for the back of the Iowa state quarter, which would be issued in August 2004, wanted to use *American Gothic*. Though the image had appeared with proper clearance on a U.S. postage stamp in 1998, nothing says "public domain" more emphatically than a coin. VAGA and the mint weren't able to negotiate an agreement on how to assert that the image on the back of this state quarter was not the nation's common property. Instead, Wood's *Arbor Day*, which everyone agreed wasn't copyright protected, appeared on Iowa's quarter. This angered Nebraskans, since the Arbor Day holiday started there in 1872.[155]

When critics in the 1970s and early 1980s, faced with the increasing commercial exploitation of Wood's best-known painting, tried to salvage his art from the junkpile of kitsch, *American Gothic*, once an emblem of the struggle between Puritans and moderns, joined another culture war. Culminating in the 1983–1984 Wood retrospective that traveled from New York to Minneapolis, Chicago, and San Francisco, the reassessments of Wood by Matthew Baigell, James Dennis, Karal Ann Marling, and Wanda Corn provoked a backlash from conservative protectors of high culture's sanctity. The former *New York Times* art critic Hilton Kramer lambasted the exhibit and Corn's catalogue for tampering with the canon of twentieth-century American painting by trying to expand the rubric of modernism to include the regionalists and by introducing "extra-artistic standards," taking "trash" seriously, depriving the public of "any useful guidance in determining artistic quality," and enacting the "revenge of the philistines." *American Gothic* was an example of "Camp"—an amusing invitation for viewers "to feel superior," a picture so bad that they think it's good—unworthy of display in an *art* museum. Kramer blamed Sontag's "Notes on 'Camp'" for the "decline" that had reached a point where Grant Wood could get a respectful retrospective. "It severed the link between high culture and high seriousness that had been a fundamental tenet of the modernist ethos," he complained. "It released high culture from its obligation to be entirely serious, to insist on difficult standards, to sustain an attitude of unassailable rectitude." To deny *American Gothic* the status of art in the 1980s was to oppose postmodernism's blurring of the boundaries between high and mass culture— boundaries crucial to the very conception of modernist art as a realm free from the contamination of kitsch.[156]

Kramer repeated the accusation that "a more virulent version" of Wood's regionalism had been "official government policy in Stalin's Russia and Hitler's Germany" and honored "the lonely band of modernists" of the New York School who had struggled against provincialism, isolationism, and nativism in the 1940s and emerged triumphant in the 1950s. (The emblematic hero of this struggle was Jackson Pollock, who had repudiated the regionalist aesthetics of his teacher Thomas Hart Benton and, as his influential supporter Clement Greenberg declared, became the "most powerful painter in America" by creating nonobjective art freed from the taint of mass culture.) The efforts of the postwar avant-garde had brought about such a widespread "taste for modernist art,"

Kramer recalled, that the work of Wood and his fellow regionalists "could confidently be regarded as a dead issue for everyone but a handful of diehard provincials nursing their grievances against a cosmopolitan culture they could neither appreciate nor ignore"—until the revisionists came along in the 1970s and 1980s to try to reverse the course of cultural history. During the Cold War, as Kramer recognized, abstract expressionism had come to symbolize artistic and political freedom in opposition to Soviet totalitarianism. Defiantly individualistic, plumbing the depths of the artist's psyche, the paintings of the New York School stood in opposition to the USSR's state-mandated social realism and its American cousin, the middlebrow insipidness of paintings such as *American Gothic*.[157]

Conservatives in the Reagan-era culture wars saw their position as a defense of standards—timeless truths, moral laws, and aesthetic values—against the encroachments of relativism. This is what allowed highbrows like Kramer to make common cause with religious fundamentalists in attacking decadent art. But the alliance was a strange one. The Reagan presidency, after all, made patriotic kitsch the official culture of the United States in the 1980s, and Reagan himself undoubtedly preferred wholesome art about wholesome subjects—like *American Gothic*—to weird stuff like Jackson Pollock's drip paintings. For most Reaganites, *American Gothic* embodied rather than threatened the values that were under attack by their foes in the culture wars.

In 1936, pondering the fate of "The Work of Art in the Age of Mechanical Reproduction," the German-Jewish critic Walter Benjamin observed that "because authenticity is not reproducible," mass reproduction undermined the "authority" or the "aura" of the original. Hoping for the destruction of capitalism, seeking "to blast open the continuum of history," Benjamin welcomed this development; reproduction, he wrote, "in its most positive form, is inconceivable without its destructive, cathartic aspect, that is, the liquidation of the traditional value of the cultural heritage." Embraced by postmodernists, Benjamin was reviled by conservatives for whom the destruction of traditional cultural values was anathema. Narrowly construed, there is, of course, only one "authentic" *American Gothic*: the painting that hangs in the Art Institute. And to its high modernist critics, that painting wouldn't have been authentic even if it hadn't been reproduced, even if it hadn't entered into the inherently fake realm of mass culture. Wood's art, Kramer grumbled, was "abysmally phony in almost every respect"—"a calculated lie from start to finish," despite his "midwestern 'roots,'" his much-vaunted fetish for authentic materials (rickrack aprons and three-pronged pitchforks, for example)—"the fantasy of an emotionally retarded adolescent sensibility desperately seeking refuge from the realities of life in a dreamworld of his own invention." Leftist critics in the 1930s had similarly derided the image's distance from "reality" as they understood it. It is ironic, then, that an image blasted for its inauthenticity from opposite political points of view came through mass reproduction to assume the authenticity of folk art, the aura of genuine Americana, the authority of a national icon.[158]

Nations are constituted through the circulation of words and images. As "imagined communities," in the political theorist Benedict Anderson's phrase, they are produced and reproduced by cultural artifacts that enable people to presume an identity with an anonymous mass of others (though by no means *all* others, since national identity also depends on boundaries). "An American will never meet, or even know the names of more than a handful of his 240,000,000-odd fellow-Americans," Anderson writes. "He has no idea of what they are up to at any one time." Yet through those mass-circulated words and images—for example, TV news catchphrases such as "America Attacked" or "The Nation at War" or "America Decides"—"he" experiences the shared time and space of "a solid community."[159]

Since the 1980s, words and images have renewed and solidified the conflation of America and the "heartland." "'Heartland' appeared in so many headlines and network TV slogans during coverage of the Oklahoma City bombing" in 1995, observes the cultural critic Leslie Savan, "that The Heartland virtually became the nation's new name." In the summer of 2001, the Bush White House called the president's vacation "The Home to the Heartland Tour," a label that, Savan writes, "not so subtly drove home the point that he was relieved as hell to get out of Washington and other phony places East." With their competing bus tours of the "heartland," the 2004 presidential campaigns again revealed the bipartisan consensus that "middle America" is the "real" America. Bush's "Heart and Soul of America Tour" fired up the crowds by playing George Strait's song "Heartland" before the president told them, "The true heart and soul of America is found right here in [insert name of midwestern city or town]." (To resounding boos, he jeered John Kerry for praising entertainers at a New York fundraiser: "I'm running against an opponent who thinks the heart and soul of America is in Hollywood.") "I can't tell you how excited I am to kick off our celebration of America right here in the heartland," Kerry exclaimed in Cloquet, Minnesota. On July 4, in Wheeling, West Virginia, Dick Cheney accused Kerry of being "on the left, out of the mainstream, and out of touch with the conservative values of the heartland." That same day, in Cascade, Iowa, Kerry honored "family, responsibility and service" as "values that are rooted in the heartland." The immediate conventional wisdom after the election held that the heartland's concern for "moral values" won it for Bush.[160]

When I say that for more than seventy years—and with the proliferation of parodies, especially for the last forty—*American Gothic* has represented the nation, I mean that, like the American flag, the Bald Eagle, and the Statue of Liberty (perhaps the only national symbols that continue to surpass it in circulation), it has not only reflected but helped create American identity. And unlike those abstract symbols, *American Gothic* personifies the nation: gives it white faces, locates it in the "middle" both geographically and socioeconomically, establishes that middle as *the* national identity ("identity" literally means "sameness"), situates, by implication, other faces and places on the margins or outside. A recent homage to *American Gothic* in a dental journal—the piece ended by paying tribute to the dentistry of Dr. McKeeby—called it "the essence of middle America—a national portrait of the archetypal American family." For all the efforts to deploy the image to broaden national identity, the common point of reference, the norm, remains the "original."[161]

The heartland embraces New York after 9/11. [© The New Yorker Collection
2001 Marisa Acocella from cartoonbank.com. All rights reserved.]

Just after 9/11 *The New Yorker* published a cartoon of the
American Gothic pair wearing "I ♥ NY" T-shirts. I remember
being both moved and troubled when I saw it: moved because
it represented the outpouring of sorrow and sympathy for
the victims of the World Trade Center attacks—a collective
grief that seemed, for a moment, to suspend difference and

conflict—the faces in the cartoon looking sad, almost tender, rather than self-righteous; troubled because it suggested that "America" hadn't much liked New York before 9/11, that even in the imagination of a *New Yorker* cartoonist, "America" meant the heartland, the middle that expanded to include New York only in the aftermath of catastrophe. Or maybe the cartoon was questioning that sorrow and sympathy, depicting it as opportunistic, shallow, or facile, bought and worn as cheaply and easily as a tourist's T-shirt. In the spring of 2004, a furrowed *American Gothic* couple on the cover of the *Village Voice* represented the "paranoid nation"—uncertain, insecure, anxious—that had emerged out of 9/11 and the open-ended "War on Terror." An anti-war collage revealed that people outside the United States have also come to view "America" through *American Gothic*. In the disturbing *American Gothic 2*, Michael Dickinson, an English-born artist, novelist, and teacher living in Turkey, depicted George W. Bush and Tony Blair as smug neo-imperialists. Bush skewers maps of Iraq and Afghanistan on his pitchfork as Blair stands behind him, dressed in American drag and singing the tune of his American patron. Osama bin Laden lurks in the background: a reminder that he remained at large despite the war? an attempt to equate Bush and Blair with fundamentalist terrorists? A bomber zooms in over the house. Flames shoot up behind the gothic window.[162]

I prefer a different *American Gothic*, one in which the "they" of the framed figures have not become the "we" of the nation. Why should they? I have a print of the painting on the wall of my office, and I often pause from whatever I'm doing to look up at those faces, which glare down on me at my desk (or his does, hers staring off as if she can't stand the sight of me), prodding me with guilt to start working again. It's a creepy image, or it can be if you look at it carefully, and even though I've just tried to describe how and suggest why it came to stand for America, I'm still disturbed that "we" would want to embrace their self-righteousness, their purity, their certainty as the essence of America, as who "we" are at our best. I like ironic distance better. *Not* identifying with those grim-visaged figures may be unkind to them, but they probably wouldn't care even if they were real, and irony can rescue *American Gothic* from cliché.

Who are those people? we can ask again. Maybe we don't know them as well as we thought we did. Maybe they aren't unambiguously pious, proper, and chaste. Maybe they aren't as sure of themselves as they first appear. Maybe they do have conflicts, pleasures, torments, fancies, secrets. Maybe if we look at them as enigmas, let them confound and haunt us, we'll see them, strangely, as very much like us after all.

Grant Wood revisited *American Gothic* a year before he died, five months before *Fortune* proposed turning it into a war poster, in a letter to Nellie Sudduth, an admirer of the painting from Idaho. Wood repeated his standard line about how he hadn't intended it as satire, explained how he thought of the man and woman as father and daughter rather than husband and wife, as "basically solid and good people," and how the most important thing about the painting wasn't "the particulars" but was "whether or not these faces are true to American life and reveal something about it." But he also seemed to resist *American Gothic*'s transformation into a wholly celebratory symbol of the nation. If the particulars didn't matter as much as its general Americanness, he reveled in them anyway:

Papa runs the local bank or perhaps the lumber yard. He is prominent in the church and possibly preaches occasionally. In the evening, he comes home from work, takes off his collar, slips on overalls and an old coat, and goes out to the barn to hay the cow. The prim lady with him is his grown-up daughter. Needless to say, she is very self-righteous like her father.

What was American about them wasn't just their solidity and goodness but "their faults and fanaticism." Why deny this? Why, he suggested to Nellie Sudduth, simplify its meanings? And he pointed out the lock of the woman's hair, twisting down her neck, perhaps mirroring the snake plant on the porch to her right, that he let escape.[163]

NOTES

1. "Eldon Art Center in August; Ottumwans to Have Exhibits,"
   Ottumwa Courier, August 1, 1930, "Art Center to be Opened
   in Eldon," *Eldon Forum*, July 31, 1930, clippings on microfilm reel 103 in the Edward B. Rowan Papers, Archives of
   American Art, Smithsonian Institution (hereafter EBR-AAA);
   Edward B. Rowan, "The American Federation of Arts' Experiment in Cedar Rapids, Iowa," n.d., reel D–142, EBR-AAA,
   15; Edward B. Rowan to Jay Sigmund, August 13, 1930, reel
   D–141, EBR-AAA.
2. "Eldon Youth's Art on Exhibit," *Des Moines Register*, February
   1, 1931, clipping on reel 103, EBR-AAA; Rowan, "American
   Federation of Arts' Experiment," 16; Edward B. Rowan,

"Community Fine Arts," n.d., reel D–142, EBR-AAA, 2–3; Edward B. Rowan, "Report of the Little Gallery of the American Federation of Arts in Cedar Rapids, Iowa—May 1931," reel D–142, EBR-AAA, 3.

3. Wanda M. Corn, *Grant Wood: The Regionalist Vision* (New Haven: Yale University Press, 1983), 129; Harry W. Henderson, "House Painter," letter to the editor, *Wall Street Journal*, July 18, 1986, 21; "Grant Wood: McKinley Teacher," http://www.cedar-rapids.k12.ia.us/mcKinley/Wood.html; Dorothy Dougherty, "The Right and Wrong of America: Grant Wood's 'American Gothic' Is Finally Understood," *Cedar Rapids Gazette*, September 6, 1942, clipping in Nan Wood Graham (hereafter NWG), unnumbered scrapbook, Figge Art Museum, Davenport, Iowa (hereafter FAM); Darrell Garwood, *Artist in Iowa: A Life of Grant Wood* (New York: W. W. Norton, 1944), 119.

4. "Eldon, Iowa," tourist brochure; http://www.netins.net/show case/eldon/ghouse.html; Nan Wood Graham with John Zug and Julie Jensen McDonald, *My Brother, Grant Wood* (Iowa City: State Historical Society of Iowa, 1993), 73; James M. Dennis, *Grant Wood: A Study in American Art and Culture* (Columbia: University of Missouri Press, 1986), 80.

5. John Carter, *Solomon D. Butcher: Photographing the American Dream* (Lincoln: University of Nebraska Press, 1985); Wanda M. Corn, "The Birth of a National Icon: Grant Wood's American Gothic," *The Art Institute of Chicago Centennial Lectures: Museum Studies 10* (Chicago: Contemporary Books, 1983), 256, 258. Some of Butcher's photographs, though not the Curry portrait, were published in his *Pioneer History of Custer County, Nebraska* (Denver: The Merchants Publishing Company, 1901) and *Sod Houses or the Development of the Great American Plains* (Kearney, Neb.: Western Plains Publishing Company, 1904).

6. Hazel E. Brown, *Grant Wood and Marvin Cone: Artists of an*

Era (Ames: Iowa State University Press, 1972), 32; NWG, *My Brother*, 73–74; NWG, "Why My Brother Painted 'American Gothic,'" *Magazine Digest*, May 1944, 45–48, excerpted in Julie Jensen McDonald, *Grant Wood and Little Sister Nan: Essays and Remembrances* (Iowa City: Penfield Press, 2000), 44; Courtney Donnell, notes from NWG visit to Art Institute of Chicago, July 1980, Department of American Art, Art Institute of Chicago (hereafter AIC-DAA); Byron McKeeby, quoted in Joan Liffring-Zug, *This Is Grant Wood Country* (Davenport, Iowa: Davenport Municipal Art Gallery, 1977), 5.

7. NWG, *My Brother*, 74.

8. This paragraph is indebted to the painstaking analysis in James S. Horns and Helen Mar Parkin, "Grant Wood: A Technical Study," in *Grant Wood: An American Master Revealed*, ed. Brady M. Roberts, James M. Dennis, James S. Horns, and Helen Mar Parkin (Rohnert Park, Calif.: Pomegranate Art Books, 1995), 69–72.

9. H.S.M. [Harlan S. Miller], "Over the Coffee," *Des Moines Register*, January 12, 1935, 16, clipping in NWG, scrapbook 2, FAM; http://www.gardenadvice.com/index.cfm/fuseaction/basics .detail /basicsId/106580/catId/31259.

10. "Paintings by Grant Wood Accepted for American Exhibition," *Cedar Rapids Gazette*, October 28, 1930, clipping in microfilm scrapbooks, Archives, Art Institute of Chicago (hereafter AIC-A); "High Society and Plain 'Bohemians' Mix at Art Show," *Chicago Post*, October 30, 1930, clipping in microfilm scrapbooks, AIC-A; *The Art Institute of Chicago Report for the Year 1930* (Chicago: Art Institute of Chicago, 1931), 84; Percy Eckhart to Allan McNab, February 10, 1964, Curatorial Files, AIC-DAA.

11. Donald E. Gettings, quoted in Bill Richards, "Plan to Brave the Crowds at Eldon? Better Take Along a Sleeping Bag," *Wall Street Journal*, June 27, 1986, sec. 2, 29.

12. Larry D. Hatfield, "Hard Times Foreclosing on the American

Dream," *San Francisco Examiner*, February 23, 1986, A–1, A–6; "An Iowa Town Debates the Fate of the Grant Wood's *Gothic* Backdrop," *People*, September 7, 1987, 111.

13. Vernon Jones, quoted in Richards, "Plan to Brave," 29; Mildred Manning Oral History Interview, April 13, 1990, State Historical Society of Iowa; McDonald, *Grant Wood and Little Sister Nan*, 41. The description of the decayed house comes from an unidentified newspaper article quoted by McDonald.

14. Carl Smith, quoted in "'Gothic' Gift," *Des Moines Register*, February 17, 1991, 2B; Bruce Thiher, telephone interviews, July 9, 2001, and July 8, 2004.

15. http://www.grantwoodstudio.org/.

16. "Grant Woodn't: Roseanne and Tom Arnold Plan an Iowa Xanadoozy," *People*, November 25, 1991; Courtney Graham, "Courtney's State Facts: Iowa," http://www.usatrip.org, posted 1996.

17. Donnell, quoted in Richards, "Plan to Brave," 29; Don DeLillo, *White Noise* (New York: Viking, 1985), 12–13; Thiher interviews.

18. Park Rinard and Arnold Pyle, "The Work of Grant Wood," *Catalogue of the First New York Exhibition of Paintings and Drawings by Grant Wood, With an Evaluation of the Artist and His Work* (New York: Ferargil Galleries, 1935), 3–4.

19. "Grant Wood Dies: Famed Artist, 50," *New York Times*, February 13, 1942, sec. 1, 21; "Grant Wood to Be Buried Saturday at Anamosa, Scene of His Boyhood," *Iowa City Press-Citizen*, February 13, 1942, 1; "Artist Grant Wood Dead," *Daily Iowan*, February 13, 1942, 1; "Iowa's Painter," *Time*, February 23, 1942, 65; NWG, *My Brother*, 9–17.

20. Garwood, *Artist in Iowa*, 33 and passim; NWG, *My Brother*, 19–30; Liffring-Zug, *This Is Grant Wood Country*, 63.

21. Brady M. Roberts, "The European Roots of Regionalism: Grant Wood's Stylistic Synthesis," in Roberts, Dennis, Horns,

and Parkin, *Grant Wood*, 1–2; Corn, *Grant Wood*, 28–29, 30; NWG, *My Brother*, 64.

22. Helen J. Hinrichsen, quoted in Liffring-Zug, *This Is Grant Wood Country*, 22; Corn, *Grant Wood*, 31, 70.

23. Thiher interview, July 9, 2001.

24. "The culture of the copy muddies the waters of authenticity," writes Hillel Schwartz in *The Culture of the Copy: Striking Likenesses, Unreasonable Facsimiles* (New York: Zone Books, 1996), 377. But authenticity also depends on copying. "[W]orks of art achieve the status of original only through reproduction," Susan Lambert points out in *The Image Multiplied: Five Centuries of Printed Reproductions of Paintings and Drawings* (London: Trefoil, 1987), 13.

25. I spent Sunday, June 13, 2004, in front of the real thing. I'd seen it before, of course, but I decided I ought to devote a day to observing visitors' reactions to it. I tried to be unobtrusive, but I did get some quizzical looks. What could I be writing in my notebook?

26. Park Rinard, "Grant Wood," NBC radio script, "Art for Your Sake" series, April 27, 1940, in NWG, scrapbook 3, FAM. Emphasis Rinard's.

27. Addams's cartoon originally appeared in the November 25, 1961, issue of *The New Yorker* and is reprinted in *The World of Charles Addams* (New York: Knopf, 1991), 181. The conversation was overheard by Alice and Dave Denison at the Art Institute of Chicago on May 8, 2004, and reported verbatim to me on an *American Gothic* postcard.

28. "Grant Wood Dies," *Art Digest*, February 15, 1942, 18; "An Iowa Secret," *Art Digest*, October 1, 1933, 6; H. L. E. [Harry L. Engle], "Now Then–," *Palette & Chisel*, January 1931, clipping in NWG, scrapbook 1, FAM.

29. On rotogravure sections, see Frank Luther Mott, *American Journalism: A History of Newspapers in the United States*

Through 260 Years: 1690 to 1950 (New York: Macmillan, 1950), 684. On wire transmission of pictures, see Alfred McClung Lee, *The Daily Newspaper in America: The Evolution of a Social Instrument* (New York: Macmillan, 1937), 531–36. The color version appeared as part of an insert in a cover story titled "U.S. Scene," *Time*, December 24, 1934, 24–26.

30. Mrs. Earl Robinson, "An Iowa Farm Wife Need Not Look Odd," *Des Moines Register*, November 30, 1930, sec. 10, 6, and Mrs. Inez Keck and Mrs. Ray R. Marsh, quoted in "Snatches from the Mail," *Des Moines Register*, December 14, 1930, sec. 10, 6, both clippings in NWG, scrapbook 1, FAM.

31. "Grant Wood Here: Farm Wives Irked by His Paintings," *Omaha World-Herald*, March 4, 1931, clipping in NWG, scrapbook 1, FAM; quoted in "Iowans Get Mad," *Art Digest*, January 1, 1931, 9.

32. "American Gothic," *Hammond Times*, November 17, 1930, clipping in microfilm scrapbooks, AIC-A.

33. Wood, quoted in "American's Painting Rouses Ire of His Fellow Iowans," *Chicago Leader*, December 26, 1930, clipping in microfilm scrapbooks, AIC-A, and in "Iowans Get Mad," 9; "Open Forum," *Des Moines Register*, December 21, 1930, quoted in Dennis, *Grant Wood*, 85.

34. "Grant Wood, Iowa Artist, Receives a Flood of Praise," *Des Moines Register*, December 28, 1930, sec. 10, 6 [the paper listed the incorrect date of December 21 on this page]; Dennis, *Grant Wood*, 85.

35. Edward B. Rowan, "The Artists of Iowa," *Cedar Rapids Gazette*, November 7, 1930, clipping in NWG, scrapbook 1, FAM; "What the Woman Who Posed Says," *Des Moines Register*, December 28, 1930, sec. 10, 6; McDonald, *Grant Wood and Little Sister Nan*, 72; NWG, "Why My Brother Painted 'American Gothic,'" 47; NWG, *My Brother*, 46.

36. *Webster's Collegiate Dictionary* (Springfield, Mass.: G. & C.

Merriam, 1929), 825. On the history of the gothic, and the literary gothic in particular, I am indebted to Richard Davenport-Hines, *Gothic: Four Hundred Years of Excess, Horror, Evil and Ruin* (New York: North Point Press, 1999), and Cathy N. Davidson, *Revolution and the Word: The Rise of the Novel in America* (New York: Oxford University Press, 1986), esp. chap. 8. On the contemporary gothic, see Mark Edmundson, *Nightmare on Main Street: Angels, Sadomasochism, and the Culture of the Gothic* (Cambridge: Harvard University Press, 1997).

37. http://www.iowahistory.org/sites/gothic_house/gothic_house .html; John E. Seery, "Grant Wood's Political Gothic," *Theory & Event* 2:1 (1998), 9, 8, 11, and passim.

38. *American Gothic*, dir. John Hough, VHS, Vidmark Entertainment, 1988.

39. Garwood, *Artist in Iowa*, 73, 91, quoted in Seery, "Grant Wood's Political Gothic," 13–14; Seery, "Grant Wood's Political Gothic," 14; NWG, *My Brother*, 149.

40. Thomas Wolfe, *Look Homeward, Angel* (1929; New York: Scribner, 1995), 498.

41. *The Rocky Horror Picture Show*, dir. Jim Sharman, 1975, DVD, Fox Home Entertainment, 2000; John Kilgore, "Sexuality and Identity in *The Rocky Horror Picture Show*," in *Eros in the Mind's Eye: Sexuality and the Fantastic in Art and Film*, ed. Donald Palumbo (Westport, Conn.: Greenwood Press, 1986), 151–59.

42. Ken D. Trivette, "You Might Want to Hold Off on the Judging," http://members.aol.com/KenTBC/SermonPage23.html, downloaded July 17, 2001.

43. Caption to reproduction of *American Gothic*, *Christian Science Monitor*, November 8, 1930, and "Grant Wood Here," clippings in NWG, scrapbook 1, FAM; Eleanor Jewett, "American Paintings, Sculpture Exhibition Will Be Open Today," *Chicago Tribune*, October 30, 1930, clipping in microfilm

scrapbooks, AIC-A; "Iowans Get Mad," 9; "Art and Artists," *Chicago American*, December 16, 1930, clipping in microfilm scrapbooks, AIC-A.

44. Walter Prichard Eaton, "American Gothic," *Boston Herald*, November 14, 1930, clipping in NWG, scrapbook 1, FAM; quoted in Michael Solomonson, "Walter Prichard Eaton," *American National Biography*, ed. John A. Garrity and Mark C. Carnes (New York: Oxford University Press, 1999), vol. 7, 266.

45. Christopher Morley, "The Bowling Green," *Saturday Review of Literature*, January 17, 1931, 533; Joan Shelley Rubin, *The Making of Middlebrow Culture* (Chapel Hill: University of North Carolina Press, 1992), 138.

46. Stein's comments were reported by her friend Rousseau Voorhies in a lecture in June 1934. See "Rousseau Voorhies, Traveler, Lecturer, Visits at Montrose," *Montrose* [Iowa] *Mirror*, n.d., n.p., and "Gertrude Stein Admires Grant Wood, Iowa Artist," *Des Moines Register*, June 17, 1934, clippings in NWG, scrapbook 1, FAM, and untitled clipping about Voorhies and Stein from the *Chicago Tribune*, October 1934, on microfilm reel 2424 in the Maynard Walker Gallery Papers, Archives of American Art. The account of the S.P.C.S. and Stein's near visit to Iowa City is from Frank Luther Mott, *Time Enough: Essays in Autobiography* (Chapel Hill: University of North Carolina Press, 1962), 138–45.

47. H. W. Janson, "Benton and Wood, Champions of Regionalism," *Magazine of Art*, May 1946, 199; Matthew Baigell, *The American Scene: American Paintings of the 1930's* (New York: Praeger, 1974), 110; Corn, "Birth of a National Icon," 255.

48. Robert Hughes, *American Visions: The Epic History of Art in America* (New York: Knopf, 1997), 439, 442; Seery, "Grant Wood's Political Gothic," 6–7, 11–12, 23; Dougherty, "Right and Wrong of America."

49. Arthur Millier, "Bible Belt Booster," *Los Angeles Times Sun-*

day Magazine, April 7, 1940, 14–15, in NWG, scrapbook 4, FAM.

50. George Hutchinson, *The Harlem Renaissance in Black and White* (Cambridge: Harvard University Press, 1995), 313; F. Scott Fitzgerald to H. L. Mencken, October 7, 1920, in *Correspondence of F. Scott Fitzgerald*, ed. Matthew J. Bruccoli and Margaret M. Duggan (New York: Random House, 1980), 70; H. L. Mencken, "American Culture" (June 1920), reprinted in *A Mencken Chrestomathy* (New York: Alfred A. Knopf, 1949), 178, 180.

51. H. L. Mencken, "The Sahara of the Bozart" (1917; expanded 1920), in *Chrestomathy*, 185, 184; Fred C. Hobson, Jr., *Serpent in Eden: H. L. Mencken and the South* (Chapel Hill: University of North Carolina Press, 1974), 32 and passim.

52. Mencken, "Sahara," 195; H. L. Mencken, "Puritanism as a Literary Force" (1917), quoted in Fred Hobson, *Mencken: A Life* (New York: Random House, 1994), 192; Harold E. Stearns, "Preface," *Civilization in the United States: An Inquiry by Thirty Americans*, ed. Harold E. Stearns (New York: Harcourt, Brace, 1922), vii; Warren I. Susman, "Uses of the Puritan Past" and "The Frontier Thesis and the American Intellectual," in *Culture as History: The Transformation of American Society in the Twentieth Century* (New York: Pantheon, 1984), 45–47, 36.

53. Douglas Clayton, *Floyd Dell: The Life and Times of an American Rebel* (Chicago: Ivan R. Dee, 1994), 38, 24; Barbara Ozieblo, *Susan Glaspell: A Critical Biography* (Chapel Hill: University of North Carolina Press, 2000), 37–39; Susan Glaspell, *The Road to the Temple* (New York: Frederick A. Stokes, 1927), 193; Floyd Dell, *Homecoming: An Autobiography* (New York: Farrar & Rinehart, 1933), 149, 170, 128; George Cram Cook, quoted in Glaspell, *Road*, 202.

54. Robert Hullihan, "Grant Wood's America," *Des Moines Regis-*

ter Sunday Magazine, October 2, 1983, 13; William L. Shirer, *20th Century Journey: A Memoir of a Life and the Times*, vol. 1, *The Start, 1904–1930* (New York: Simon and Schuster, 1976), 171.

55. Shirer, *20th Century Journey*, 185–86.

56. Carl Van Vechten, *The Tattooed Countess: A Romantic Novel with a Happy Ending* (New York: Alfred A. Knopf, 1924), 184, 229, 24, 109, 180, 78, 76, 162. The real-life counterpart of the Countess was Mahala Dutton Benedict Douglas, whose husband owned Quaker Oats. When young Carl told her that he was so bored with Cedar Rapids he'd "like to put on a bath towel and run through the streets naked," she gave him a towel and said "Go ahead." She and her husband were on the *Titanic* in 1912. He died; she survived. See Bruce Kellner, *Carl Van Vechten and the Irreverent Decades* (Norman, Okla.: University of Oklahoma Press, 1968), 15–16.

57. M. K. [MacKinlay Kantor], "K's Column," *Des Moines Tribune-Capital*, December 29, 1930, clipping in NWG, scrapbook 1, FAM. Ellipses Kantor's.

58. Wood, quoted in Garwood, *Artist in Iowa*, 88; Brown, *Grant Wood and Marvin Cone*, 43 and passim; NWG, *My Brother*, 55. See also Corn, *Grant Wood*, 21.

59. "The Foothold of Art in Iowa," *Des Moines Register*, April 7, 1932, clipping on reel D–141, EBR-AAA; Jay Sigmund to Edward B. Rowan, March 19, 1931, and May 30, 1931, reel D–141, EBR-AAA; Edward B. Rowan, "Community Fine Arts," n.d., reel D–142, EBR-AAA.

60. Frederick Newlin Price, "The Making of an Artist," *New York Herald Tribune*, January 20, 1935, 21, clipping on microfilm reel 864 in the Marian S. Mayer Papers, Archives of American Art (hereafter MSM-AAA); Millier, "Bible Belt Booster," 14. Nan Wood Graham remarks that Price's article is "full of errors" in NWG, scrapbook 2, FAM.

61. Ruth Suckow, "The Top of the Ladder" and "A Pilgrim and a Stranger," in *Iowa Interiors* (New York: Knopf, 1926), 106, 155; Ruth Suckow, "Iowa," *American Mercury*, September 1926, 45; Quick, quoted in Lewis Atherton, *Main Street on the Middle Border* (Bloomington: Indiana University Press, 1954), 122. See also "A Rural Community" in *Iowa Interiors*, in which a journalist returns to his hometown of Walnut only to become less "sure of the superiority of his life" away from its "deep quietude" (171, 184).

62. Arthur Millier, "Layman and Critic Hail 'Grass Roots' Portrait," *Los Angeles Times*, July 17, 1932, part 3, 6; NWG, *My Brother*, 75.

63. Shirer, *20th Century Journey*, 275.

64. Mencken, quoted in William H. Nolte, *H. L. Mencken: Literary Critic* (Middletown, Conn.: Wesleyan University Press, 1964), 235; Eaton, "American Gothic"; "Iowan's Art the Vogue," *Kansas City Star*, n.d. [probably 1932], clipping in NWG, scrapbook 1, FAM.

65. Sinclair Lewis, *Main Street* (1920; New York: Library of America, 1992), 460, 36, 287, 475.

66. Lewis, *Main Street*, 289, 285, 287, 370, 114.

67. Hobson, *Mencken*, 229; Corn, *Grant Wood*, 114–17; Corn, "Birth of a National Icon," 264; Mencken, quoted in Nolte, *H. L. Mencken: Literary Critic*, 234; Wood, quoted in Irma Rene Koen, "The Art of Grant Wood," *Christian Science Monitor*, March 26, 1932, 6; H. L. E., "Now Then—."

68. Grant Wood to Sinclair Lewis, July 10, 1937, Sinclair Lewis Papers, Beinecke Library, Yale University; "What Thinking People Read," *Boston Evening Transcript*, July 22, 1939, clipping in NWG, scrapbook 3, FAM. Nan Wood Graham noted her brother's visits with Sinclair Lewis beneath a September 25, 1937, letter from Lewis to Wood, in scrapbook 5, FAM.

69. Edward B. Rowan, "The Artists of Iowa," *The Spotlight of*

Rotary, November 8, 1930, clipping on reel D–141, EBR-AAA; Cedar Rapids Kiwanis Club newsletter, n.d., "The Little Gallery," *Cedar Rapids Savings Letter*, July 1928, clippings on reel 103, EBR-AAA; David Turner, quoted in Edward B. Rowan to Frederick P. Keppel, November 6, 1939, reel 1366, Marvin Cone Papers, Archives of American Art; Mr. and Mrs. S. V. Shouka to Edward B. Rowan, February 1931, reel D–141, EBR-AAA. Keppel was president of the Carnegie Corporation, which had initially funded the Little Gallery.

70. Harvey Green, *The Uncertainty of Everyday Life, 1915–1945* (New York: HarperCollins, 1992), 6, 18; Lynn Dumenil, *The Modern Temper: American Culture and Society in the 1920s* (New York: Hill and Wang, 1995), 148. The Saks Fifth Avenue ad appeared in *The New Yorker*, August 7, 2000, 1.

71. Robert S. Lynd and Helen Merrell Lynd, *Middletown: A Study in Modern American Culture* (New York: Harcourt, Brace & World, 1929), 7–8, 139, 138n; George Barton Cutten, *The Threat of Leisure* (New Haven: Yale University Press, 1926), 89.

72. Lewis, *Main Street*, 287.

73. Corn, *Grant Wood*, 88; Frederick Lewis Allen, *Only Yesterday: An Informal History of the Nineteen-Twenties* (New York: Harper & Brothers, 1931), 88–89.

74. Carl Van Vechten, "The Folksongs of Iowa" (1918), in *Sacred and Profane Memories* (New York: Alfred A. Knopf, 1932), 30; Van Vechten, *Tattooed Countess*, 129, 231.

75. Millier, "Layman and Critic."

76. John E. Findling, *Chicago's Great World's Fairs* (Manchester and New York: Manchester University Press, 1994), 72, 68, 89, 103; Charles E. Hendry, *Youth Inspects the New World* (New York: Association Press, 1933), 27; *Century of Progress: Chicago World's Fair Souvenir* (Chicago: Arena Company, 1933), n.p.

77. Robert B. Harshe, "Foreword," in *Catalogue of A Century of Progress Exhibition of Paintings and Sculpture, Lent from American Collections* (Chicago: Art Institute of Chicago,

1933), xiii; Inez Cunningham, quoted in "Art Exhibit Proof of City's Rise, Says Critic," *Chicago Tribune*, May 21, 1933, clipping in microfilm scrapbooks, AIC-A; Findling, *Chicago's Great World's Fairs*, 114; Virginia Gardner, "Art Institute Attracts 11,000; 2,000 View Whistler's Mother," *Chicago Tribune*, May 31, 1933, "'Mother' is Most Popular Painting," *New York News*, November 3, 1933, "Whistler's 'Mother' Was Fair's Popular Lady," *Columbus Dispatch*, November 3, 1933, clippings in microfilm scrapbooks, AIC-A; "Visiting America's Greatest Exhibition of Paintings," *Official World's Fair Weekly*, May 13, 1933, folder 16–132, Century of Progress International Exposition Records, Special Collections, Richard J. Daley Library, University of Illinois-Chicago (hereafter CPR).

78. Robert B. Harshe, "Foreword," in *Catalogue of A Century of Progress Exhibition of Paintings and Sculpture, 1934* (Chicago: Art Institute of Chicago, 1934), ix.

79. Press Release, Promotion Department, A Century of Progress, May 28, 1933, folder 1-930, CPR; Beulah Donohue, "Whistler's 'Mother' to be at Fair," *Milwaukee Sentinel*, February 5, 1933, "Experts Praise Art Collection," *Chicago Leader*, July 14, 1933, "Chicago Fair Art Visitors Ask for 'Whistling Mother'," *Chicago Daily News*, July 22, 1933, Cati Mount, "'Greatest Art Display' Delights Visitors at World's Fair," *Chicago Times*, May 28, 1933, clippings in microfilm scrapbooks, AIC-A.

80. "Art Displays Prove Popular," *Chicago Leader*, September 1, 1933, "Ohio Contributed Greatest Number of Noted Paintings to Display at Chicago Fair," *Dayton Herald*, May 29, 1933, "Art Exhibit Attracts Wide Interest Among Chicago World Fair Patrons," *Providence Tribune*, June 10, 1933, clippings in microfilm scrapbooks, AIC-A; C. J. Bulliet, *Art Masterpieces in a Century of Progress Fine Arts Exhibition at the Art Institute of Chicago* (Chicago: Sterling North, 1933), n.p.

81. Thomas Craven, "Grant Wood, of Iowa," *Chicago Herald-*

American, January 2, 1935, clipping in NWG, scrapbook 4, FAM; Bulliet, *Art Masterpieces*, n.p. This claim about print sales at A Century of Progress appeared in Ruth Pickering, "Grant Wood, Painter in Overalls," *North American Review*, September 1935, 275.

82. Millier, "Layman and Critic"; caption to "This Picture, 'American Gothic' (1930)," *Des Moines Register*, March 3, 1940, clipping in microfilm scrapbooks, AIC-A.

83. Bruce Bliven, "A Century of Treadmill," *New Republic*, November 15, 1933, 11–12. The statistics are from David M. Kennedy, *Freedom from Fear: The American People in Depression and War, 1929–1945* (New York: Oxford University Press, 1999), 163.

84. Robert W. Rydell, *World of Fairs: The Century-of-Progress Expositions* (Chicago: University of Chicago Press, 1993), 115, 9.

85. Bliven, "Century of Treadmill," 12; "First Lady at Art Institute," *Chicago Herald and Examiner*, November 1, 1933, clipping in microfilm scrapbooks, AIC-A; Eleanor Roosevelt to Edith Lehman, November 7, 1933, and Eleanor Roosevelt to Elinor Morgenthau, November 4, 1933, in *The Papers of Eleanor Roosevelt, 1933–1945* [microfilm], ed. Susan Ware and William H. Chafe (Frederick, Md: University Publications of America, 1986), reels 13 and 8.

86. Rydell, *World of Fairs*, 215.

87. Malcolm Vaughan in the *New York American*, quoted in "New York Criticism: Grant Wood in the East," *Art Digest*, May 1, 1935, 18; Gilbert Seldes, "Notes and Queries," *Today*, May 18, 1935, 16; Gilbert Seldes, "The Great American Face," *Esquire*, July 1943, 80; "An Iowa Artist Discovers Iowa," *Literary Digest*, August 13, 1932, 13; Albert Shaw, "The Progress of the World," *Review of Reviews*, January 1935, 15, clipping in NWG, scrapbook 2, FAM; "Grant Wood," *Scholastic*, October 22, 1932, 1, clipping in NWG, scrapbook 1, FAM. The *Liter-*

ary Digest and *Scholastic* articles are the earliest I have found that see *American Gothic* as celebrating the "pioneer spirit."

88. Stephen Alexander, "White Haired Boy of the Crisis," *New Masses*, May 7, 1935, 28; Curtis Harnack, *We Have All Gone Away* (Ames: Iowa State University Press, 1981), 125, 132–33; Dorothy Schwieder, "Iowa: The Middle Land," in James H. Madison, ed., *Heartland: Comparative Histories of the Midwestern States* (Bloomington: Indiana University Press), 290. Ellipses Alexander's.

89. Francis Robert White, "Revolt in the Country," reprinted in *Artists Against War and Fascism: Papers of the First American Artists' Congress*, ed. Matthew Baigell and Julia Williams (New Brunswick, N.J.: Rutgers University Press, 1986), 192.

90. Lincoln Kirstein, "An Iowa Memling," *Art Front*, July 1935, 6, 8; John Steuart Curry, "What Should the American Artist Paint?" (originally published as "Curry's View: What Should the American Artist Paint?" *Art Digest*, September 1935, 29) and Joe Jones, "Gropper 1940" (from the American Contemporary Art Galleries' William Gropper exhibition catalog, 1940), reprinted in *Social Realism: Art as a Weapon*, ed. David Shapiro (New York: Frederick Ungar, 1973), 109, 209; James Johnson Sweeney, "Grant Wood," *New Republic*, May 29, 1935, 76–77.

91. Corn, "Birth of a National Icon," 255. Another East Coast critic asserted in 1935 that *American Gothic* "stopped short of satire" but also "failed to lead us on toward pity or tenderness for his models"—as victims of Puritanism or the Depression?—and to tell whether they are "loveable folk or not." Pickering, "Grant Wood, Painter in Overalls," 275.

92. Harold Stearns and Matthew Josephson, quoted in Steven Biel, *Independent Intellectuals in the United States, 1910–1945* (New York: New York University Press, 1992), 107–108.

93. Wood, quoted in "Grant Wood Dies," *Art Digest*, February 15,

1942, 18; "Grant Wood Appointed Art Director for Encyclopedia," *Iowa Press Citizen*, April 30, 1941, clipping in microfilm scrapbooks, AIC-A; "Wood Works," *Time*, April 22, 1935, 56; Thomas Craven, "Grant Wood," *Scribner's*, June 1937, 19, 22; H. L. Mencken to Grant Wood, February 2, 1940, microfilm reel 66, H. L. Mencken Papers, Manuscripts and Archives Division, New York Public Library, Astor, Lenox and Tilden Foundations. Permission granted by the Enoch Pratt Free Library, Baltimore, in accordance with the terms of the bequest of H. L. Mencken. If Wood answered Mencken's letter, his reply has not survived.

94. Dennis, *Grant Wood*, 152; Seldes, "Notes and Queries," 16; Rinard and Pyle, "The Work of Grant Wood," 10; "Art: Son of the Soil Masters Painting Before Showing N.Y.," *Newsweek*, April 20, 1935, 20. The autobiography was never written.

95. Edwin Valentine Mitchell, *Concerning Beards* (Hartford: Finlay Press, 1930), 83; "Wood Works," 56; Corn, *Grant Wood*, 3; Wood, quoted in Liffring-Zug, *This Is Grant Wood Country*, 53, 27; Grant Wood, handwritten comment on "A Definition of Regionalism," November 16, 1937, in NWG, scrapbook 2, FAM; Thomas Hart Benton, *An Artist in America* (New York: Robert M. McBride & Company, 1937), 258, 265–66. The "flaming red beard" story became a standard part of Wood's repertoire on the lecture circuit. See, for example, "Red Beard Helped Him Get That Way, Grant Wood Says," *Minnesota Chats*, February 7, 1939, clipping in NWG, scrapbook 2, FAM.

96. Ed Cray, *Levi's: The "Shrink-to-Fit" Business That Stretched to Cover the World* (Boston: Houghton Mifflin, 1978), 82–83, 80; quoted in Kennedy, *Freedom from Fear*, 165; Barbara Melosh, *Engendering Culture: Manhood and Womanhood in New Deal Public Art and Theater* (Washington: Smithsonian Institution Press, 1991), 1, 58.

97. Millier, "Bible Belt Booster," 14.

98. Warren I. Susman, "Culture and Commitment," in *Culture as History*, 205–6.

99. Michael Denning, *The Cultural Front: The Laboring of American Culture in the Twentieth Century* (London: Verso, 1997), 128; Susman, "Culture and Commitment," 203; "Address by the Honorable Robert M. LaFollette, United States Senator from Wisconsin, on the Occasion of the Opening of the Exhibition of the Section of Fine Arts, at the Corcoran Gallery of Art, November 2, 1939, Introduced by Mr. Edward Bruce, Chief of the Section of Fine Arts," copy in *Papers of Eleanor Roosevelt*, reel 3; Corn, *Grant Wood*, 108, 148; Karal Ann Marling, *Wall-to-Wall America: A Cultural History of Post Office Murals in the Great Depression* (Minneapolis: University of Minnesota Press, 1982), 43.

100. Melosh, *Engendering Culture*, 67, 2.

101. Corn, *Grant Wood*, 94; Dennis, *Grant Wood*, 212.

102. Davenport-Hines, *Gothic*, 321; Grant Wood to Virgil M. Hancher, June 18, 1941, in Grant Wood Letters, Special Collections Department, University of Iowa Libraries, Iowa City, Iowa (hereafter UIL); Grant Wood to J. C. Reid, August 24, 1941, in J. C. Reid Papers, UIL.

103. Elizabeth Stillinger, "From Attics, Sheds, and Secondhand Shops: Collecting Folk Art in America, 1880–1940," in *Drawing on America's Past: Folk Art, Modernism, and the Index of American Design*, ed. Virginia Tuttle Clayton, Elizabeth Stillinger, Erika Doss, and Deborah Chotner (Washington: National Gallery of Art, 2002), 45–59; Cahill, quoted in Erika Doss, "American Folk Art's 'Distinctive Character': The Index of American Design and New Deal Cultural Nationalism," in *Drawing on America's Past*, 70; Constance Rourke, "American Art: A Possible Future," *American Magazine of Art*, July 1935, 398 (reprinted in Constance Rourke, *The Roots of American Culture and Other Essays* [New York: Harcourt, Brace, 1942], 275–96); Constance Rourke, *Charles Sheeler: Artist in the American Tradition* (New York: Harcourt, Brace, 1938), 87; "Section of Fine Arts—Special Bulletin, The Artists Receive a

Bill of Rights, Extract from the Address by President Roosevelt at the Dedication on March 17, 1941, of the National Gallery of Art, Washington, D.C.," copy in *Papers of Eleanor Roosevelt*, reel 3; Grant Wood, *Revolt Against the City* (Iowa City: Clio Press, 1935), 39. Doss argues that the *Index* was concerned with a "larger symbolic construction of national cultural identity" (64–65) and that the local and regional differences it documented were "fitted into a federally designed national blueprint focused on cultural commonality and consensus" (67).

104. Wood, *Revolt Against the City*, 18–19, 22–23, 39, 29; Nan Wood Graham, quoted in McDonald, *Grant Wood and Little Sister Nan*, 90; "Iowa Cows Give Grant Wood His Best Thoughts," *New York Herald Tribune*, January 23, 1936, 17; Craven, "Grant Wood," *Scribner's*, June 1937, 21.

105. James R. Shortridge, *The Middle West: Its Meaning in American Culture* (Lawrence: University Press of Kansas, 1989), 39, 99–100; Wood, *Revolt Against the City*, 26–27.

106. Lewis Mumford, "A Group of Americans," *The New Yorker*, May 4, 1935, 31, 28; Rourke, "American Art," 397; Lewis Mumford, *The Brown Decades: A Study of the Arts in America, 1865–1895* (1931; rpt. New York: Dover, 1971), 109. See also Robert L. Dorman, *Revolt of the Provinces: The Regionalist Movement in America, 1920–1945* (Chapel Hill: University of North Carolina Press, 1993), 53.

107. Marling, *Wall-to-Wall America*, 89.

108. Rydell, *World of Fairs*, 56–58; Susman, "The People's Fair: Cultural Contradictions of a Consumer Society," in *Culture as History*, 219.

109. "A Conversation with Gordon Parks," in Martin H. Bush, *The Photographs of Gordon Parks* (Wichita, Kans.: Edwin A. Ulrich Museum of Art, 1983), 36, 38; Gordon Parks, *Voices in the Mirror: An Autobiography* (New York: Doubleday, 1990), 65, 78–79, 81–83; Gordon Parks, *Half Past Autumn: A Retro-*

spective (Boston: Little, Brown, 1997), 28, 30, 32.

110. "A Portfolio of Posters," *Fortune*, August 1941, 79; Dougherty, "Right and Wrong of America," and "Grant Wood Sees Artists in Significant Role in Defense," *Iowa City Press-Citizen*, May 3, 1941, clippings in NWG, unnumbered scrapbook, FAM.

111. *Chicago Tribune*, May 4, 1943, 4. Ellipses in original.

112. Albert O. Olson, *Stopping at Grant Wood's "American Gothic"* (Chicago: Joseph K. Arnold, 1944), n.p.

113. Meredith Willson, *The Music Man* (New York: G. P. Putnam's Sons, 1958), 28.

114. Willson, *Music Man*, 26, 74.

115. "Pied Piper of Broadway," *Time*, July 21, 1958, 42, 44, 46.

116. These characterizations come from Bernard Rosenberg, "Mass Culture in America" (1957), Dwight Macdonald, "A Theory of Mass Culture" (1953), Clement Greenberg, "Avant-Garde and Kitsch" (1939), and Irving Howe, "Notes on Mass Culture" (1948), all collected in Bernard Rosenberg and David Manning White, eds., *Mass Culture: The Popular Arts in America* (New York: Free Press, 1957), 9, 59–73, 98–107, 496–503; and Dwight Macdonald, "Masscult & Midcult," in *Against the American Grain* (New York: Random House, 1962), 3–75.

117. Clement Greenberg, Letter to the Editor, *The Nation*, March 16, 1946, reprinted in Greenberg, *The Collected Essays and Criticism: Volume 2, Arrogant Purpose, 1945–1949*, ed. John O'Brian (Chicago: University of Chicago Press, 1986), 64; Macdonald, "Masscult & Midcult," 39, 43; Mary Morsell, "Grant Wood," *Art News*, April 27, 1935, 13.

118. Dorothy Odenheimer, "Grant Wood Winning Posthumous Honors," *Chicago Sun*, November 8, 1942, Fritzi Weisenborn, "Grant Wood . . . Isolationist Art," *Chicago Sunday Times*, November 15, 1942, clippings in microfilm scrapbooks, AIC-A; John Fabian Kienitz, "Grant Wood," *Art in America*, January 1943, 49–50.

119. Bulliet, quoted in "Grant Wood Show Stirs Praise, Ire," *Des*

Moines Register, December 20, 1942, clipping in microfilm scrapbooks, AIC-A; NWG, handwritten note, unnumbered scrapbook, FAM.

120. Weisenborn, "Grant Wood . . . Isolationist Art"; Odenheimer, "Grant Wood Winning Posthumous Honors"; Peyton Boswell, "The Grant Wood Controversy," *Art Digest*, December 1, 1942, 3.

121. H. W. Janson, "The International Aspects of Regionalism," *College Art Journal*, May 1943, 114–15; Janson, "Benton and Wood, Champions of Regionalism," 184–86, 200.

122. Thomas Craven, "Our Decadent Art Museums," *American Mercury*, December 1941, 687, 685, 684; "Mr. Headache to the Arts," *Newsweek*, December 20, 1943, 82; Harry S. Truman, Diary, April 4, 1948, June [21?], 1956, in *Off the Record: The Private Papers of Harry S. Truman*, ed. Robert H. Ferrell (Columbia: University of Missouri Press, 1980), 129, 336; George Dondero, "Modern Art Shackled to Communism," *Congressional Record*, House, 81st Congress, 1st Session, vol. 95, parts 8–9 (August 16, 1949), 11584–87.

123. Thomas Craven, "From September Morn to American Gothic," *Saturday Evening Post*, November 6, 1943, 101; J. J. Lankes, "Let Grant Wood Alone," *Art Digest*, December 15, 1942, 4; "Chicago Honors Memory of Grant Wood," *Art Digest*, November 1, 1942, 6; Peyton Boswell, "Grant Wood," *Art Digest*, February 15, 1942, 3; Bourke Hickenlooper, quoted in "Hickenlooper Praises Grant Wood's Work," *Iowa City Iowan*, October 29, 1942, clipping in microfilm scrapbooks, AIC-A (typed copy of speech on reel 864, MSM-AAA); "Grant Wood: Iowa's No. 1 Artist Who Died Last Winter Gets Big Retrospective Show in Chicago," *Life*, January 18, 1943, 52.

124. "High-Brow, Low-Brow, Middle-Brow," *Life*, April 11, 1949, 99. Lynes's original article, "Highbrow, Middlebrow, Lowbrow: Which Are You?.," appeared in the February 1949 issue of *Harper's*.

125. "Priceless Paintings You Can Afford," *American Weekly*, April 25, 1959, clipping in NWG, scrapbook 4, FAM.

126. Thomas Suchomel and Mrs. Edward A. O'Neal, letters to the editor, *Cedar Rapids Gazette*, n.d., clippings in NWG, scrapbook 12, FAM; Matthew Baigell, "Grant Wood Revisited," *Art Journal* 26, 2 (Winter 1966–67), 116.

127. Len Glasser, telephone interview, August 12, 2003; Amid Amidi, "A Corny Start to the Week," April 7, 2003, http://www.animationblast.com/news/apr03/. Thomas Frank has analyzed this kind of advertising in *The Conquest of Cool: Business Culture, Counterculture, and the Rise of Hip Consumerism* (Chicago: University of Chicago Press, 1997).

128. "The Masterpiece," *The Dick Van Dyke Show*, originally aired October 2, 1963, DVD, Season 3, Disc 1, Image Entertainment, 2003.

129. "Oliver Buys a Farm," *Green Acres*, originally aired September 15, 1965, on CBS, Museum of Television and Radio, New York; Gerard Jones, *Honey, I'm Home! Sitcoms: Selling the American Dream* (New York: St. Martin's, 1992), 167.

130. Jones, *Honey, I'm Home!*, 165.

131. Jones, *Honey, I'm Home!*, 166; David Marc, *Comic Visions: Television Comedy and American Culture*, 2nd ed. (Malden, Mass.: Blackwell, 1997), 67; "American Gothic On Television and Off," *TV Guide*, April 20, 1968, 32, 33; Irene Ryan to Nan Wood Graham, n.d., NWG, scrapbook 6, FAM.

132. "American Gothic On Television and Off," 33.

133. Susan Sontag, "Against Interpretation" (1964) in *Against Interpretation and Other Essays* (1966; New York: Picador, 2001); Linda Hutcheon, *A Theory of Parody: The Teachings of Twentieth-Century Art Forms* (New York and London: Routledge, 1985), 33, 57, 52.

134. "Who Changed the Picture of the Farmer's Wife?" *U.S. News & World Report*, March 13, 1961, 73; Nixon, quoted in Elaine

Tyler May, *Homeward Bound: American Families in the Cold War Era* (New York: Basic Books, 1988), 17. According to the S&H website, "by the 1960's, S&H was the largest purchaser of consumer products in the world. Green Stamps were everywhere." They could be redeemed for purchases from the S&H catalog, which was said to be "the largest single publication in the U.S." in 1964, with enough copies to "circle the earth 1½ times!" S&H boasts that in the same year, the company was printing three times more stamps than the U.S. post office. See http://www.greenpoints.com/info/inf_aboutsh.asp.

135. http://www.newmansownorganics.com.

136. "American Gothic On Television and Off," 34; Ellen Feldman, "Till Divorce Do Us Part," *American Heritage*, November 2000, 47; "Who's That Girl?" *American Heritage*, April 2001, 16.

137. Alfred Gescheidt, telephone interview, August 21, 2002.

138. The Carter cartoon, by Mike Peters, originally appeared in the *Dayton Daily News*. It is in the collections and online catalog of the Library of Congress, Prints and Photographs Division.

139. "ERA Yes" was produced by the League of Women Voters and can be found in the collections and online catalog of the Library of Congress, Prints and Photographs Division. "God Bless America and Please Hurry" and Tom Till's "Meltdown!" are reproduced in Corn, *Grant Wood*, 137, 138.

140. "Up the Establishment" is reproduced in Gary Yanker, *Prop Art* (New York: Darien House, 1972), 225, and can be found in the collections and online catalog of the Library of Congress, Prints and Photographs Division.

141. Gescheidt interview; Harriet Van Horne, "Johnny Carson: The Battle for TV's Midnight Millions," *Look*, July 11, 1967, 81; Kelly Riordan, "*Playboy* Gothic," *Playboy*, October 1967, 12.

142. NWG, "In Answer to Interrogatory," handwritten statement, scrapbook 7, FAM; "Two Magazines, TV Show Sued for $9 Mil-

lion," *Los Angeles Times*, May 1, 1968, 3; "'American Gothic' Widow Sues Over Caricatures," *New York Times*, May 2, 1968, 94; "A Gothic Tale," *Newsweek*, May 13, 1968, 35; "People," *Time*, May 10, 1968, 51; Letters to the editor, quoted in McDonald, *Grant Wood and Little Sister Nan*, 58. Nan's appearance on *To Tell the Truth* was taped on October 20, 1970. See NWG, scrapbook 16, FAM, and McDonald, *Grant Wood and Little Sister Nan*, 108.

143. "'Sister Nan' Adds Dash of Humor to the Grant Wood Art Tradition," *Cedar Rapids Gazette*, September 20, 1942, clipping on reel D–256, Associated American Artists Papers, Archives of American Art; "Modish Sister of Grant Wood Amused by Some Caricatures," *Des Moines Register*, November 12, 1972, 2B.

144. Donnell, notes from NWG visit to Art Institute of Chicago; NWG, "Law Suit," typed statement, May 16, 1968, scrapbook 14, FAM; Albin Krebs, "Notes on People," *New York Times*, April 28, 1978, A18; Eileen Keerdoja with Ronald Henkoff, "The 'Gothic' Model Keeps a Vigil," *Newsweek*, December 8, 1980, 17–18; "Personalities," *Washington Post*, October 21, 1981, B4; Meg Cox, "You'd Be Sour, Too, If You Were Subject of Countless Spoofs," *Wall Street Journal*, May 18, 1983, 1; McDonald, *Grant Wood and Little Sister Nan*, 57–58.

145. Quoted in John Harlow, "Meet the Bubbleheads," *London Times*, December 7, 2003, 16. The spokesman, described as a "television executive," isn't named in the article.

146. Breyer, quoted in Arlen W. Langvardt and Kyle T. Langvardt, "Unwise or Unconstitutional? The Copyright Term Extension Act, the Eldred Decision, and the Freezing of the Public Domain for Private Benefit," *Minnesota Intellectual Property Review*, vol. 5, no. 2 (2004), 228, http://mipr.umn.edu/archive/v5n2/Langvardt.pdf; Dennis S. Karjala, "Opposing Copyright Extension: A Forum for Information on Congress's Recent

Extension of the Term of Copyright Protection and for Promoting the Public Domain," http://homepages.law.asu.edu/~dkar jala /OpposingCopyrightExtension/.

147. The U.S. Copyright Office database is at http://www.copy right.gov/records/. See also an inconclusive exchange about *American Gothic*'s copyright status on the website of the Coalition for Networked Information at http://www.cni.org/Hforums/cni-copyright/2000-02/.

148. Robert Panzer, interview, July 9, 2004, VAGA, 350 Fifth Avenue, Suite 2820, New York, NY 10118. Those seeking permission to use *American Gothic* for commercial uses should direct their inquiries to this address. Nan's will is discussed in McDonald, *Grant Wood and Little Sister Nan*, 132.

149. Panzer is cited on the right of publicity in John Busbee, "What's Missing Here? Why? American Gothic Has an Image Problem," *Artscene*, August 2004, 11. The California statute can be found at http://caselaw.lp.findlaw.com/cacodes/civ/3344-3346.html.

150. Busbee, "What's Missing Here?," 10, 11. The article's title refers to *Artscene*'s unwillingness to seek permission to use *American Gothic* as an illustration.

151. Pam Ryan to A. James Speyer, February 5, 1976, Speyer to Ryan, May 3, 1976, in AIC-DAA.

152. Hillary Chura, "Coors Hikes Spending on Gay Ads," *Advertising Age*, March 27, 2000, 16; "Ken," Fort Smith, Arkansas, and "Thomas," Lincoln, Nebraska, "Visitor Comments" on "New 'American Gothic,' " http://www2.commercialcloset.org/cgi-bin/iowa/portrayals.html?record=246; Bill Husted, "Tiff Brewing Over Coors' Choice of Artwork in Ad," *Denver Post*, March 30, 2000, 2; Ellen Warren and Terry Armour, "Gay or Not, 'Gothic' Couple Can't Sell Beer," *Chicago Tribune*, March 31, 2000, 2. "The Commercial Closet" is a website that collects gay advertising.

153. E-mail from Stephanie Astrow, June 12, 2003.

154. John Steinbeck, *The Grapes of Wrath* (1939; rpt. New York: Penguin, 1992), 572; Vicki Goldberg, *The Power of Photography: How Photographs Changed Our Lives* (New York: Abbeville Press, 1991), 136.

155. Panzer interview; Michael Kelly, "Two Bits for Iowa May Beat Nebraska," *Omaha World-Herald*, June 24, 2003, 1b; "Vilsack Unveils Iowa Quarter Design," July 17, 2003, http://www.governor.state.ia.us/news/2003/july/july1703_1.html.

156. Hilton Kramer, "The Return of the Nativist," *New Criterion*, October 1983, 58, 63, reprinted in *The Revenge of the Philistines: Art and Culture, 1972–1984* (New York: Free Press, 1985), 51–59. Kramer's remarks on Sontag are in "Postmodern: Art and Culture in the 1980s," in *Revenge of the Philistines*, 8. On modernism's and postmodernism's relationships to mass culture, see Andreas Huyssen, *After the Great Divide: Modernism, Mass Culture, Postmodernism* (Bloomington: Indiana University Press, 1986).

157. Kramer, "Return of the Nativist," 59; Greenberg, quoted in Erika Doss, *Benton, Pollock, and the Politics of Modernism: From Regionalism to Abstract Expressionism* (Chicago: University of Chicago Press, 1991), 374. See also Serge Guibaut, *How New York Stole the Idea of Modern Art: Abstract Expressionism, Freedom, and the Cold War*, trans. Arthur Goldhammer (Chicago: University of Chicago Press, 1983), and Erika Doss, "The Art of Cultural Politics: From Regionalism to Abstract Expressionism," in Larry May, ed., *Recasting America: Culture and Politics in the Age of Cold War* (Chicago: University of Chicago Press, 1989), 195–220.

Doss explicitly rejects Kramer's restrictive definition of modernism as "avant-garde abstraction" and seeks to expand the term to include Benton's efforts "to fuse art and life . . . through energetic and open-ended forms" (*Benton, Pollock, and the*

Politics of Modernism, 10). James Dennis similarly argues for the regionalist triumvirate's shared modernist commitment "to eliminate the traditional divisions between elite and popular subject matter" and to "pluralism," "change and chance" in opposition "to the closed, deterministic world of nineteenth-century positivism." See James M. Dennis, *Renegade Regionalists: The Modern Independence of Grant Wood, Thomas Hart Benton, and John Steuart Curry* (Madison: University of Wisconsin Press, 1998), 5.

158. Walter Benjamin, "The Work of Art in the Age of Mechanical Reproduction" (1936), in *Illuminations*, ed. Hannah Arendt, trans. Harry Zohn (New York: Schocken, 1968), 243n, 221; Walter Benjamin, "Theses on the Philosophy of History" (1940), in *Illuminations*, 262; Kramer, "Return of the Nativist," 61.

159. Benedict Anderson, *Imagined Communities: Reflections on the Origin and Spread of Nationalism*, rev. ed. (London, New York: Verso, 1991), 26.

160. Leslie Savan, "Move Over 'Heartland,' Here Comes 'Homeland,'" *Salon*, October 1, 2001, http://archive.salon.com/people/feature/2001/10/01/homeland/; see, for example, "President's Remarks in Canton, Ohio," July 31, 2004, http://www.whitehouse.gov/news/releases/2004/07/20040731-2.html; John Kerry, "Celebrating the Spirit of America," July 2, 2004, http://www.johnkerry.com/pressroom/speeches/spc_2004_0702.html; Mike Allen, "Cheney Says Kerry's Voting Record Shows He Is Out of Touch with the Heartland," *Washington Post*, July 4, 2004, A11; "Kerry Celebrates Fourth of July in America's Heartland," press release, July 4, 2004, http://www.johnkerry.com/pressroom /releases/pr_2004_0704.html.

161. Eric K. Curtis, "Homage to the Heartland," *Inscriptions: Journal of the Arizona Dental Association* 11, 7 (January 1998), 31, online at http://www.dentaleditors.org/Article%20Library/curtis %20art3.htm.

162. The "I ♥ NY" cartoon is the work of Marisa Acocella, *The New Yorker*, October 15, 2001, 54; "Paranoid Nation," *Village Voice*, May 26–June 1, 2004; Michael Dickinson, *American Gothic 2*, http://carnival_of_chaos.tripod.com, reprinted in *Peace Signs: The Anti-War Movement Illustrated*, ed. James Mann (Zürich: Edition Olms Zürich, 2004), 88.

163. Grant Wood to Nellie B. Sudduth, March 21, 1941, http://www.campsilos.org/mod2/students/wood_letter.htm. Camp Silos is a site dedicated to documenting "our agricultural heritage."

INDEX

Page numbers in *italics* refer to captions;
page numbers after 173 are endnotes.